PREPARING *for* MARRIAGE

PREPARING
for MARRIAGE

CONVERSATIONS TO HAVE BEFORE SAYING "I DO"

DAVID *and* MEG ROBBINS
GENERAL EDITORS

with TIM GRISSOM *and* TRACY LANE

BETHANYHOUSE

a division of Baker Publishing Group
Minneapolis, Minnesota

© 2023 by FamilyLife

Published by Bethany House Publishers
Minneapolis, Minnesota
www.bethanyhouse.com

Bethany House Publishers is a division of
Baker Publishing Group, Grand Rapids, Michigan

Printed in the United States of America

Library of Congress Cataloging-in-Publication Data
Names: Robbins, M. David, Jr., editor. | Robbins, Meg, editor.
Title: Preparing for marriage : conversations to have before saying "I do".
Other titles: Preparing for marriage (Bethany House Publishers)
Description: Minneapolis, Minnesota : Bethany House Publishers, a division of Baker Publishing Group, 2023. | Introduction signed by David and Meg Robbins, president & CEO of FamilyLife. | Includes bibliographical references.
Identifiers: LCCN 2021048809 | ISBN 9780764239496 (trade paper) | ISBN 9780764240669 (casebound) | ISBN 9781493436057 (ebook)
Subjects: LCSH: Marriage—Religious aspects—Christianity—Study and teaching.
Classification: LCC BV835 .P726 2023 | DDC 248.8/44—dc23/eng/20211008
LC record available at https://lccn.loc.gov/2021048809

New content for the 2023 edition provided in part by Shelby Abbott, Janel Breitenstein, and Tracy Lane

Contributors to the 1998 and 2010 editions: Dennis Rainey, David Boehi, Brent Nelson, Jeff Schulte, and Lloyd Shadrach

Cover design by Greg Jackson, Thinkpen Design, Inc.

Cover photography ©Priscilla Du Preez

23 24 25 26 27 28 29   7 6 5 4 3 2 1

To Dennis & Barbara Rainey,
who shaped the first edition of this resource
that forged a foundation for our marriage
more than twenty years ago.

CONTENTS

PREPARING FOR MARRIAGE

A Note from David and Meg Robbins

First things first: Congratulations on your engagement! Marriage is one of life's craziest, most exhilarating adventures! It is wonderful, yet deeply challenging. It is fun and exciting, but it takes a lot of hard work. It's also a holy space, and it exposes the hard and unknown places in our hearts. Marriage is soul-to-soul, skin-to-skin intimacy, and sometimes it will frustrate you more than you can ever imagine. Marriage is sometimes a lot of sex, sometimes a lot of disappointment. Marriage is a lot of things!

Most importantly for you, *your* marriage is . . . about to get real.

You're no longer thinking in terms of somedays or maybes because now there's a ring on the finger and a date on the calendar. Soon you'll put to the test everything the memes and the influencers, your friends and family, and the books and podcasts have told you about marriage.

Since you're reading this book, you're ready. But are you prepared?

A few months from now, the wedding will be behind you. Your honeymoon trip will be a collection of memories (hopefully a lot of good ones). The gifts will have been opened and placed on the kitchen counter, a living room shelf, the closet (let's be honest), or returned to the store (more honesty). And, marking the true end of the wedding season, the last thank-you will have been mailed (please don't ask how long this took us).

Once that day comes, we really don't want you feeling the regret of having planned a great wedding but having done little to prepare for a great marriage. As we like to say at our FamilyLife Weekend to Remember conferences, "Great marriages don't just happen."

Speaking of FamilyLife and marriage conferences, can we tell you something about us and why we believe in this book? We actually don't like to consider ourselves marriage experts. Yes, we've been married for more than two decades, and we lead a large ministry helping families find connection with each other and with God. Though we've walked alongside countless couples, immersed ourselves in the study of marriage, both theologically and psychologically, and spend many of our waking hours thinking and talking about marriage, we don't come at you with edicts and prescriptions but as those who journey with you and who still need to ask for forgiveness daily from the people we love the most.

We come to you as a couple still working on making our marriage better, day in and day out, and want to help you do the same.

Here's what we know: Marriage takes work, intentionality, and . . . help. Marriage will take more than just the two of you.

After all, think of the entourage it takes just to make even a tiny wedding happen, from the florist to the musicians to making the toast at the reception. And if a wedding takes that much help, how much more does a thriving marriage?

So don't go it alone. (Marriage or this book!)

We can't do the work for you, but we want to walk beside you with the intentionality and the help-for-your-marriage part. And yet we're just the names on the front of this book. We hope you have a real-life mentor couple sitting across from you, helping you think through these conversations. If you don't have someone yet, we have some tips on how to invite a couple whose marriage you admire to walk with you during this season and throughout your marriage (see page 159 for a QR code with tips for finding a mentor couple). Trust us, you'll want someone to call after the first married fight who can remind you it's normal! You'll need someone to grab coffee with when you know you should apologize but you really want your spouse to go first. You'll want someone in your marriage's corner when it feels easier to sleep at your mom's house for the night.

As excited as we are to walk this path with you, we also don't want to overpromise anything. This book will not enable you to detour around every conflict. You won't find a decision tree or fancy formula that painlessly converts every difference of opinion into one-hundred-percent agreement. And no mentor couple will have any hidden, century-old secrets for how to make it to sixty-five years of marriage.

But what we can promise are guides for healthy conversations that will lay a solid foundation for your marriage—a deeper understanding of and appreciation for your differences, proven ways to face challenges, and biblical truth that will help keep your love strong for a lifetime.

God created marriage and made it a beautiful union between one man and one woman for a lifetime. Sure. You'll encounter a million little things and likely a handful of life-altering challenges that can detour your marriage—even mere hours after exchanging your vows. Still, two individual hearts fully surrendered to God's design and purposes for marriage, plus moment-by-moment individually seeking Him for the strength to defer to each other, consider each other, and stick it out together can add up to a lifetime of love and flourishing for the long run.

Let's do this! Cheering you on as you dive into these conversations and praying your marriage far surpasses your expectations! We believe it can.

David and Meg Robbins
President & CEO of FamilyLife

HOW TO MAKE THE MOST OF
PREPARING FOR MARRIAGE

We designed *Preparing for Marriage* to be much more than hypothetical theories or lectures on marriage. That's why, throughout the book, you will find exercises, interviews, and prompts for reflection and discussion. We want you to read *and interact* with the content. Please don't skip over these. They are the "secret sauce" of this book. We want to help you connect meaningfully with your fiancé,[1] not just consume more marriage content. The questions and exercises will help you discover each other, uncover your expectations, and envision a bright lifetime of pursuing what matters most—together.

In Section One, we'll set the table for the rest of the conversations in this book (and for the rest of life). Once we've established the foundation, Section Two will explore where you are both coming from—we'll take inventory of how you became who you are right now and try to uncover your expectations for your future together. Then, in Section Three, we'll talk more about where you want to go and how to get there.

We want to get you both talking about marriage—and not just marriage in general, but *your* marriage. These conversations are intended to open up specific dialogue between the two of you so you can begin to understand yourselves and each other better as you talk about your hopes, values, and expectations.

Let's get started!

1. This spelling is the male form of the term (as opposed to *fiancée*), but in this book we're using it for both men and women.

section one

THE FOUNDATION

one

LET'S TALK ABOUT WHAT MARRIAGE IS

Why are you getting married?

That's a pretty basic question. Even so, maybe you haven't really thought much about it. Maybe marriage is just the next obvious step. You love each other. You're committed to each other. You're better together. I (David) remember how intense my desire to be with Meg forever was—it was practically all I could think of in the days leading up to our engagement and wedding. I'd caught a glimpse of what life with her would be like, and I decided to chase that dream.

These are all good answers. And clearly you care about getting it right, or you wouldn't be putting in the time and effort to go through this book.

But let's step back and consider an even bigger, foundational question—not just why are *you* getting married, but . . . why marriage at all? Chances are, because you chose this book, there's a value of faith in your relationship.

If you believe, as we do, that God designed marriage, maybe it makes sense to you that learning more about His design is a good place to start preparing for your own marriage.

1. Take a moment to consider this question: What do you believe are God's purposes for creating marriage?

   ....

   ....

The Story of Eric and Amanda

Who would have ever thought that Eric, an athlete and outdoorsman, and Amanda, a refined and accomplished woman, would wind up falling in love? They met while skiing with a group of friends in the Rocky Mountains in Colorado. The moment Eric saw Amanda, he approached her and asked her out. Amanda was intrigued that someone would be so bold, and she accepted.

For the rest of the week, they found themselves enthralled with each other's company. They skied together, shared meals, sipped hot chocolate, and talked about anything they could think of. It all felt so natural, so easy, like they belonged together.

Both Eric and Amanda had dated in the past, and Eric had even been engaged. But they both knew that what they were now experiencing was different. After they returned to their homes, three hundred miles apart, they carried on a long-distance relationship. Over the next few months, they talked nightly on the phone, often for hours, and texted like teenagers constantly in communication. They even managed to spend several weekends together.

It felt natural for Eric, who was twenty-eight, and Amanda, who was twenty-six, to think seriously about marriage.

Even before meeting Amanda, Eric believed that the most important thing to know before he got married was that his future bride would be compatible with him. He wanted to find someone who was attractive and fun to be with. He also longed for a wife who enjoyed fishing, was willing to give him the freedom to be with his buddies, and was a natural in the kitchen.

Amanda also had expectations about marriage and the kind of guy she wanted to marry. She dreamed of marriage as a fulfilling, romantic adventure with the man she loved. He would be sensitive, attractive, well organized, and would share the home responsibilities. He would express his feelings, be a good listener, and provide security. He would enjoy children as much as she did and be a loving, caring father.

Because they had strong feelings for each other, Eric and Amanda were more than willing to please each other. Eric would often be vulnerable when he talked with Amanda, telling her about his struggles and doubts as well as his victories. He was a gentleman, creative with romantic gestures, and listened attentively to all that Amanda had to say. He even took her to the theater—a stretch for Eric-the-outdoorsman! Amanda was convinced: *This is the man of my dreams. We're perfect for each other. We hardly ever argue.*

Amanda had never gone fishing before meeting Eric, but now she found herself spending weekends at a lake, casting for bass by his side. She would attend his softball games and even cheer for Eric's favorite basketball team. Everything seemed fun when they spent time together. And Eric could not believe his taste buds when he ate Amanda's cooking. He knew, *This woman is like me in so many ways, and she is thoughtful and caring toward me.*

Of course, no two people are exactly alike, and that was the case with Eric and Amanda. He was boisterous, outgoing, and loved to be around lots of people. She was much more reserved; she enjoyed spending time with a few close friends but felt uncomfortable at a large party. She loved to read, while he streamed TV shows to relax.

Their families were quite different: Eric's dad was an auto mechanic, and his mother a waitress. Amanda's parents were divorced, but her father, a wealthy attorney, provided well for all of them. This gap between their backgrounds asserted itself most when they visited their prospective in-laws.

When she lay in bed at night, Amanda had to admit she was a little bothered about the difference in the depth of their religious convictions. She attended her church regularly; her belief in God was important. Eric said he had never enjoyed church and didn't attend on his own. But he did seem to enjoy going with her when he visited on weekends. That gave Amanda hope that he would eventually change and desire the same faith she had. All things considered, she thought, they seemed perfect for each other.

They were both tired of being single, and by now they couldn't stand to be apart. They couldn't imagine spending life without each other.

And so, while Amanda was enjoying her family's traditional Fourth of July weekend at a resort, she looked out one evening and saw Eric standing by the lake. She ran to say hi; he dropped to one knee. "Will you marry me?"

19

Their engagement was four months—just enough time to arrange the wedding. The final weeks were hectic. Amanda moved to Eric's city and started a new job while also setting up the wedding in her hometown. They met with Amanda's pastor and received some advice about marriage, and they found a home and began moving in.

The ceremony itself raced by in a blur, and suddenly they found themselves reciting their vows: "With this ring I thee wed . . . in sickness and in health, in poverty or in wealth, till death do us part."

Happily ever after, here they came . . .

2. What parts of this story—if you'd been present—would raise concerns for you?

_____

_____

3. How would you have answered if this couple had approached you and asked, "Do you think we are ready to get married?"

_____

_____

In many ways, Eric and Amanda may be a superb match. Yet, there are some potential challenges that come to mind. There were significant gaps in their knowledge and expectations, and most of the time before they married was spent hundreds of miles apart. They were so caught up in emotions and infatuation that they failed to work out some crucial issues before they committed their lives to each other.

Their family backgrounds and upbringing were worlds apart, and Amanda's parents' divorce wasn't something the couple talked about to determine the impact on Amanda or what mistakes they could avoid. They also had not really discussed their compatibility on faith and some of life's deeper issues.

In fact, they seemed to have different goals for their marriage altogether.

Despite their strong feelings for each other, Eric and Amanda were beginning their marriage in the dark. They didn't understand the bigger picture of marriage, and they knew little about how to keep their marriage together after their expectations weren't fully met and their feelings started to fizzle.

God's Purposes for Marriage

God designed marriage for something bigger than "happily ever after." Please don't miss the promise of that statement. God wants something even bigger and better for your marriage than what you want for it.

Some may think that by starting with God when discussing marriage, we're going to shrink the thrill and delight of it all. But the opposite is true. When you understand and commit to following God's design, you'll experience greater unity and joy than you thought possible—not because you tacked God's ideas onto *your* plan, but because you *rooted* your marriage in *His* plan. God really does have your best interests at heart.

So let's dig into what God had in mind for us when He created marriage.

Marriage Models the Unity of God

In How God Relates to Himself

In Genesis, God's culminating act of creation was humanity—man and woman.

> Then God said, "Let us make man in our image, after our likeness." . . . So God created man in his own image, in the image of God he created him; male and female he created them.
>
> Genesis 1:26–27

Question: Was God talking to Himself? When He said, "Let *us* make man in *our* image," who was on the other end of the conversation?

Yes, God was talking to Himself. Without diving into the deep waters of theology, this is the first place where the Bible identifies God as a triune being. As the storyline of the Bible continues, it becomes more and more clear that God exists in three persons: the Father, the Son, and the Holy Spirit.

Before anything on earth existed, God had a flawless, intimate community. A diverse partnership.

The marriage of two image bearers, loving each other intimately in their uniqueness, reflects the beautiful relationship enjoyed by the Trinity. Marriage is an embodied testimony, both to the couple and to the world, of God's love—a taste-it-smell-it-feel-it image of the "us" and "our" of the Trinity.

In How God Longs to Relate to Us

Ephesians refers back to Genesis 2:24 to draw an important connection:

> "Therefore a man shall leave his father and mother and hold fast to his wife, and the two shall become one flesh." This mystery is profound . . . it refers to Christ and the church.
>
> Ephesians 5:31–32

Marriage is a way of displaying the great lengths to which God has gone to pull us into closeness with Him. Jesus, represented by the groom, and the Church (Christians), represented by the bride, foster a committed relationship marked by love, faithfulness, respect, humility, service, and mercy.

Through its very nature, marriage proclaims the gospel. Your relationship will model the persevering love of Christ for His people—and the way they love Him in response.

Your marriage will be opportunity after opportunity to experience God's love and commitment in the middle of your kitchen, your bout with the flu, your craving for warmth in the middle of the night. Marriage is giving yourself to someone, warts and all. There is no greater love than that which God initiated to humankind through Jesus Christ. You may have heard it before:

> For God so loved the world, that he gave his only Son, that whoever believes in him should not perish but have eternal life.
>
> John 3:16

God wants you to know Him intimately; He has designed marriage to be a clear and trustworthy image of His devoted and sacrificial love. The marriage you enter into for life will remind you and communicate to the world the lengths God went to in order have a tangible, forever relationship with His people.

4. List some ways that your marriage can model God's unity.

_____

_____

_____

_____

Marriage Is a Space to Pursue Lifelong Companionship

Soon after God created man, He said, "It is not good that the man should be alone; I will make him a helper fit for him" (Genesis 2:18). Up to this point, God had looked over each part of creation and said that it was good. But not this time. Something more was needed. Adam shouldn't be alone.

5. No sin or flaw was in the world yet, and Adam had God Himself as his companion. Why do you think it wasn't good for Adam to be alone?

_____

_____

God created in Adam a unique need in his *aloneness* that was not filled by His personal presence. Adam experienced God in the midst of perfection, yet Adam was still *alone*.

But God actively solved Adam's problem.

Now out of the ground the Lord God had formed every beast of the field and every bird of the heavens and brought them to the man to see what he would call them. And whatever the man called every living creature, that was its name. The man gave names to all livestock and to the birds of the heavens and to every beast of the field. But for Adam there was not found a helper fit for him. So the Lord God caused a deep sleep to fall upon the man, and while he slept took one of his ribs and closed up its place with flesh. And the rib that the Lord God had taken from the man he made into a woman and brought her to the man.

Genesis 2:19–22

23

6. What did God do to address Adam's need for companionship?

_____

_____

Notice that God did much more than give Adam someone so that he wouldn't be lonely. God's solution for Adam's need was to make him "a helper fit for him." It's important to note that *helper* does not mean *inferior person*. The sense of a woman's worth and role is elevated throughout the Old Testament by calling her by the same name used sixteen times for God Himself (see Psalm 30:10 and 54:4) and in other biblical references to describe the giving or absence of military help (Isaiah 30:5; Ezekiel 12:14; Daniel 11:34). To be called a helper spoke to the fact that God had plans for Adam that he could not fulfill without a spouse.

Adam needed Eve.

Also notice that this passage does not imply that every unmarried person is incomplete without a spouse. All of us are created in the image of God (see Genesis 1:26–27) and bring renown to God when we yield ourselves to His purpose and plan for our lives. Jesus, after all, was single, and God provided other intimate companionship for Him. However, in God's timing, He does sovereignly choose to bring a husband and wife together for them to accomplish together what they couldn't have accomplished apart.

7. Think of some married couples you know well. In what ways do their differences complement each other?

_____

_____

_____

Most happily married couples could point to specific examples of how God has fit them together. My (Meg) natural inner clock impels me to slow down and pay attention to the inner worlds of those I love. David tends to run through life at a fast pace and sometimes exhausts himself with well-meaning, good things. I so appreciate David's big-picture vision, and he has repeatedly told me how grateful he is for the way I encourage him to pursue goals in a healthier way.

For other couples we know, the husband is people-oriented and the wife is task-oriented. He helps her relate socially to others; she keeps him focused on tasks they need to complete.

In wisdom, God brings two people together to supplement, enhance, and shape each other. They are stronger as a team. They are two independent people who choose to become *interdependent*—this unity that reflects the Trinity also helps us better live for His purposes. How about that for a win-win?

8. As you look at your relationship, in what ways are you different and in what ways are you alike? Describe some ways that your differences already make you stronger as an interdependent team. In ways you're similar, note how these can also start to form the subculture of your family unit, and could form potential weaknesses, too.

_____

_____

_____

_____

_____

Mark this, because you'll be tempted to doubt it when things get hard down the road: Your spouse is God's gift to you. We know "Two are better than one, because they have a good reward for their toil. For if they fall, one will lift up his fellow" (Ecclesiastes 4:9–10). Keep your eyes peeled for ways your spouse continually makes you a better person—even when the growing pains can scream otherwise. How do they bring out the best in you?

Marriage Is a Unique Way to Influence the Next Generation

What if we told you your marriage, and its story, could change the world?

And no, we don't mean that together you'll start an international non-profit organization that ends the food crisis or come upon a cure for cancer while you're gardening. That stuff would be cool, but as followers of Jesus— whether single or married—your story matters in bringing God's Kingdom here and now. As it stands, He's intricately planned you and your fiancé's zip codes, memories, fascination with mountain biking or music festivals, your in-laws-to-be—even that weird sense of humor you share—to pull you toward Him and serve and love people around you (check out Acts 17:26–27).

> But you will receive power when the Holy Spirit has come upon you, and you will be my witnesses in Jerusalem and in all Judea and Samaria, and to the end of the earth.
>
> Acts 1:8

Your marriage will have power for its mission as you learn to listen and respond to the Holy Spirit. It's easier when you both feed an alertness to how He's working—say, in that conversation at the food truck or in your apartment's stairwell—pulling you to join Him together.

Rest assured, He's got a bigger vision, a bigger movement that He's orchestrating. He works through the ripples of your individual and mutual areas of influence to effect a worldwide wave of the Kingdom of God.

You don't have to be president of a Christian ministry to make waves either—while I (David) will never take for granted the thousands our work at FamilyLife affects, I also have a feeling that it's the behind-the-scenes stuff that brings the biggest smiles to God's all-seeing face. The late nights talking with my son in the dark about his fears, the extra hour I spent after school drop-off listening to a discouraged dad, the rolling of our elderly neighbor's trash bins back up her driveway every Thursday.

Your indoor soccer team, your cynical coworker, your landlord—all are authored with a purpose. Your future marriage carries the opportunity to lean into a movement that's sweeping every tribe, tongue, and nation and that stretches for generations.

One obvious way to influence the next generation: become parents! Foster, adopt, have biological children. In that way, the fruit of your relationship with God multiplies exponentially as time plods on.

Returning to the book of Genesis, where God gave direction and vision to Adam and Eve, the first couple, we read:

> And God blessed them. And God said to them, "Be fruitful and multiply and fill the earth and subdue it, and have dominion over the fish of the sea and over the birds of the heavens and over every living thing that moves on the earth."
>
> Genesis 1:28

9. Acknowledging this can be a painful subject for some: This passage makes it clear that God's design for marriage includes having kids. What do you think God had in mind when He made this a priority?

_____

_____

_____

_____

_____

IF YOU ALREADY HAVE CHILDREN

"I advocate for biological parents spending one-on-one time with their kids before and after a new marriage because it helps reassure children that they haven't completely lost their parent."

—Ron Deal, *Preparing to Blend*

10. Check out the following passages from the book of Psalms. What do you hear about God's opinion of kids and why they are important? What values of His will your marriage share?

> *Behold, children are a heritage from the LORD, the fruit of the womb a reward. Like arrows in the hand of a warrior are the children of one's youth. Blessed is the man who fills his quiver with them! He shall not be put to shame when he speaks with his enemies in the gate.*
>
> Psalm 127:3–5

> *He established a testimony in Jacob and appointed a law in Israel, which he commanded our fathers to teach to their children, that the next generation might know them, the children yet unborn, and arise and tell them to their children, so that they should set their hope in God and not forget the works of God, but keep his commandments.*
>
> Psalm 78:5–7

Part of God's intent is for every married couple (and every person) to "make disciples of all nations" (Matthew 28:19) in this generation and those to come. Psalm 78 and passages like Deuteronomy 6:2–7 (below) make it clear that the family is one of the best environments in which this can happen.

This imperative can also be broadened to being "spiritual parents"—mentor kids in your community, be your nieces' and nephews' most invested aunt or uncle. Impact any child God brings across your path.

11. Think about your life experience and the experiences of others. Why do you think God places such great emphasis on fathers and

28

mothers passing on truth to their children and to other kids God brings into their life?

12. As a couple, what are your current thoughts on having kids? Where do your biggest resistances or obstacles lie—and why? When you look at the Bible as a whole, how does this influence your thinking? What do you need to explore further?

13. If a couple is not able to have biological children (or in some cases, chooses not to), what are some ways they can influence the next generation in knowing and living for God?

. . . that you may fear the LORD your God, you and your son and your son's son, by keeping all his statutes and his commandments, which I command you, all the days of your life, and that your days may be long. Hear therefore, O Israel, and be careful to do them, that it may go well with you, and that you may multiply greatly, as the LORD, the God of your fathers, has promised you, in a land flowing with milk and honey.

Hear, O Israel: The LORD our God, the LORD is one. You shall love the LORD your God with all your heart and with all your soul and with all your might. And these words that I command you today shall be on your heart. You shall teach them diligently to your children, and shall talk of them when you sit in your house, and when you walk by the way, and when you lie down, and when you rise.

Deuteronomy 6:2–7

God's original plan called for the homes of those who love Him to be greenhouses of sorts—nurturing centers where we all seek Him and learn character, values, integrity, and what it means to grow in a relationship with Him. In no other setting does a child learn more about how to live and relate to God. At the same time, while parents have the unique gift of time with their children that no one else has, we all have been impacted by other adults who went out of their way to love and mentor us.

You may be thinking that with the inclusion of God and His plans for you to serve others, your marriage is getting pretty crowded. But what we've seen God do over and over for people who choose to make Him the foundation of their marriage and then serve Him together has been to bring a greater closeness to the marriage than they imagined. The way of godly marriage is not to live only for each other's good, but to remain open to God's leading and to be aware of ways your constant journeying with Him can spill over to impact your corner of God's world (don't miss John 15:5–11 on this).

Summary

Your future marriage will exist for more than just two people making each other happy. This isn't an exhaustive list of how God will use your marriage, but it's a start. The bottom line is that you have the opportunity and call to represent God together. And others, especially the generation coming after you, need your godly influence. To build a marriage according to His design, you cannot ignore its spiritual foundation and purposes.

Why marriage? If you can answer that question biblically now, you've got a lot going right already.

IF YOU ARE A PARENT AND HAVE BEEN MARRIED BEFORE

"A second or subsequent wedding for a parent brings three potentially competing emotional attachments into collision with one another: the couple's marriage, the child's loyalty to their family of origin, and the new blended family."

—Ron Deal, *Preparing to Blend*

two

LET'S TALK ABOUT WHAT COMMUNICATION IS

Communication is connection.

When we hear the word *communication*, many dismiss the need for improvement based on the idea that it simply refers to talking. But there is so much more to it than that.

Whether your last conversation (. . . or argument) was about takeout or the weirdness at work, there's a lot more going on than just talking.

It's crucial to take time to intentionally cultivate a healthy set of communication norms in your engagement that will bear fruit in your marriage—if both of you are committed to crafting these norms with humility and intentionality.

In the same way that making exercise a priority both *promotes* positive health outcomes (mental health, circulation, longer projected life-span) and helps *prevent* negative ones (high cholesterol, heart disease, depression, or anxiety), you'll find that the more attention you pay to healthy communication in marriage, the better your connection and intimacy will be in joyful times and the more resilient you'll be in common relationship ailments, big or small.

So when we say healthy communication, we're talking:

- understanding and being understood
- identifying a tone of voice

- detecting nonverbal cues
- responding appropriately to offense
- resolving conflict
- knowing what to say, when to say it, and how to say it
- experiencing the risks and rewards of knowing and being known
- and so much more

Again, you were both made by a personal God who values deep, authentic love and wants the two of you to enjoy nothing short of total unity. Healthy communication skills are a huge part of getting you there.

Communicating With, Not Talking At

Smartphones, texting, social media, direct messaging, and email notifications fool us into thinking we're in constant communication with people. But is communication *just* words?

Digital interaction makes it too easy to talk *at* people.

Life-giving communication requires authentic presence, being *with* someone: postures, gestures, expressions. Space for pauses and empathetic eye contact. Nuance. Stories too long to be tapped out with thumbs in a string of texts. Tell-me-more prompts to draw out the deeper realities. Feedback, warm (real-life) smiles, the passing of a tissue to wipe tears, and unrestrained dialogue without performing for an audience.

We all know how easy it can be to let digital norms shape our relationships, making it hard to be truly present. We laughed at (and had to address) some of our own communication ruts when Meg gave me a Valentine's card a few years ago. It not-so-romantically read, "There's nobody else I'd rather lie in bed and look at my phone next to . . . than you." The four-inch screen in our pocket does an amazing job of forming our habits; we have to be incredibly intentional about creating space to ask more questions, talk about what's bothering us, and dig into the hard. Don't buy into the myth that communication is about information rather than deeply knowing and being known.

Listen Up

To answer before listening—that is folly and shame.

Proverbs 18:13 NIV

The paraphrased version of this wisdom puts it quite bluntly: "Answering before listening is both stupid and rude" (Proverbs 18:13 MSG). Ouch. It stings . . . because it's true.

Listening is such an important part of the communication process, yet it's often one of the most neglected parts. If you aren't listening, you aren't communicating. If you aren't communicating, you aren't connecting. And if you aren't connecting, you are on your way to isolation.

I (David) have certainly been guilty of *listening badly* to Meg—sometimes my mind is distracted by something totally separate, or I start getting sucked into a "shame storm" of berating myself if I'm feeling defensive, or even at times I just start thinking about what I'm going to say next.

Our minds can tend to wander. So, proactive listening is one of the best methods to keep communication open (and to keep your spouse from devolving into roommate status).

Here are a few practical tips to practice *listening well* to your soon-to-be spouse:

- *Ask good questions.* Asking good questions communicates interest, and while interest is probably easy to communicate in this season of engagement, it's especially important when you're twenty years, four kids, and two demanding jobs into marriage (ask me how I know).
- *Reflectively listen* to what your spouse is trying to convey. In other words, repeat back what you hear in a way that shows you are

---

IF YOU HAVE BEEN MARRIED BEFORE

"Becoming family to one another—which is fundamentally what every blended family is hoping to accomplish—is an emotional process that requires active engagement by all parties."

—Ron Deal, *Preparing to Blend*

paying attention. You don't have to repeat everything you hear, just important points that convey you are tracking with them. Try these for example:

"What did you mean when you said _____?"

"I hear that you're saying _____. Is that right?"

- *Affirm what is being said* (aka resist the urge to list all the reasons that what they're saying is wrong). It's easy to find flaws in someone's thinking or reasoning, especially when the topic of discussion is something you are passionate about. Affirmation doesn't mean you agree with everything they're saying. Yet there are always touch points that reveal common ground, and pointing *those* out (rather than verbally jumping all over the other person) can reduce the tension and lower their guard. So after reflective listening, try something like these examples:

"I understand that you're feeling overwhelmed right now. How can I help?"

"I hear that you don't feel like I've been pulling my weight. Can we talk more through that?"

My dear brothers and sisters, take note of this: Everyone should be quick to listen, slow to speak and slow to become angry.

James 1:19 NIV

That sounds a bit utopian, doesn't it? Probably because it is incredibly hard to behave that way when we're in real relationships with people.

God's Word sets the bar high for our lives. It would be a huge bummer if the Bible said something like, "Try to listen to each other, unless, you know, your phone pings, and then obviously you have to check it real quick. If it seems like someone's not listening to you, just say it again. But LOUDER." That sounds like what the anthropology books might say about us in a few centuries, but thankfully it's not how the Bible calls us to interact with other image bearers.

Quick to listen. Slow to speak. Slow to get angry. It's a bar none of us can reach, especially in the strength of our own willpower. We have to depend on a source greater than ourselves to live this out in the ordinary, everyday grind of marriage.

But don't despair! Thankfully, if we surrender our own agenda and allow the Holy Spirit to work in and through us on a moment-by-moment basis, we tap into the ultimate power source for a life completely glorifying to God and completely exhilarating for us. Left to ourselves, we tend to walk the easier path, the path to isolation. He is the One who makes it possible for us to listen well, communicate with clarity and maturity, and focus appropriately on others so we can understand each other more fully. Daily yielding our lives to the Holy Spirit's influence in the deepest parts of us will make engagement and eventual marriage the best they can possibly be.

Listening to Understand

1. In your own words, write a listening principle found in each of the following passages of Scripture.

> *A fool takes no pleasure in understanding, but only in expressing his opinion.*
>
> *Proverbs 18:2*

Listening Principle:

_____

_____

> *Let the wise hear and increase in learning, and the one who understands obtain guidance.*
>
> *Proverbs 1:5*

Listening Principle:

_____

_____

2. What are some practical ways you could apply these listening principles in your relationship with your fiancé right now?

_____

_____

_____

_____

FOCUS ON:	RATHER THAN:
The heart behind what is being said	How you feel about what is said
The way it is being said: tone of voice, posture, etc.	The words only
Clarifying and affirming any valid points	Defense of incorrect accusations
Questions	Indictments
Understanding	Judgment

3. What's one practical way you specifically want to invest in better listening for the sake of your future marriage?

_____

_____

Speaking to Be Understood

4. In your own words, write a speaking principle found in each of the following Scripture passages.

> _Let no corrupting talk come out of your mouths, but only such as is good for building up, as fits the occasion, that it may give grace to those who hear._
>
> _Ephesians 4:29_

Speaking Principle:

_____

_____

When words are many, transgression is not lacking, but whoever restrains his lips is prudent.

Proverbs 10:19

Speaking Principle:

_____

_____

For everything there is a season, and a time for every matter under heaven . . . a time to keep silence, and a time to speak.

Ecclesiastes 3:1, 7

Speaking Principle:

_____

_____

5. What are some practical ways you'd like to apply these principles in your relationship with your fiancé right now?

_____

_____

_____

_____

In the same way a careful listener seeks clarification, we must also be deliberate about what, how, and when we choose to express ourselves.

Death and life are in the power of the tongue.

Proverbs 18:21

When we seek to speak less and listen more, we set aside self-centeredness and build togetherness, understanding another viewpoint and simultaneously seeking the best for our spouse.

Summary

Making a point to assess how you and your fiancé communicate—the extent to which you offer each other your authentic presence, listen proactively, and speak with discernment—and then taking steps to improve can be a game-changing choice for your relationship. The truth is, it will be something you'll want to continually assess and improve on, as communication in our distraction-driven world tends to naturally atrophy over time. Your future selves will appreciate beginning the habit now.

section two

WHERE WE ARE NOW

three

LET'S TALK ABOUT OUR PAST

Some of your hearts started racing when you read this chapter title. I (David) specifically remember the sick dread I carried in my stomach when I realized what I would need to share with Meg. It's true that engagement is a critical time to continue to learn each other's backstories. And that can be scary (both as the sharer and the listener). You might be wondering, *Do I have to tell my fiancé every single thing I've ever done?* Not necessarily. (Note, we'll be discussing our sexual histories more in Section Three.) Or you may be dreading the idea of recounting the ugliness of your parents' divorce. It's incredibly important, both as the one sharing and as the one listening, to maintain a spirit of grace.

These conversations can draw you together in some incredible ways. When I reflect back on having these conversations, I remember Meg's gracious acceptance of me *much more* than the dread I had going in.

You'll both want to commit to a healthy amount of listening, which will help establish a tone of understanding, compassion, and supportiveness. Besides, no matter if your past feels as picture-perfect as a 1950s TV show or if your family and past are much more soap opera–esque, we all bring a broken past into our relationships. We all have former sins—both things we've done and things that have been done to us—as well as misplaced hopes, regrets, and lies we've believed—maybe still believe—about the sacredness of a marriage relationship that can influence our future.

So it's time to open up and get more vulnerable with each other than perhaps you have previously. The exercises that follow will dig deep into your awareness and acknowledgment of where you've been.

Complete these two exercises individually first—give yourself adequate time to answer and process the questions thoughtfully and honestly. Then find a time to share your completed version with each other (armed with the healthy communication skills you've been polishing up on). This is a great spot to remind you that we recommend inviting a married couple you respect into the conversation. Sometimes just another set of attentive ears can guide your hearts and responses to process these significant conversations.

Understanding Your Personal History—A Worksheet

One of the riskiest but most rewarding aspects of a marriage relationship is the exciting experience of knowing and being known—revealing yourself and having the other person reveal themselves to you. And, as odd as it may sound, dating and engagement can sometimes work against this process. On the one hand, you want to know everything about this person. On the other hand, you may think that if this person knew everything about you, they might lose interest.

You may still be tempted to hide some specifics about your past, but we urge you not to begin your marriage by candy-coating or omitting important parts of your story. Very few of us want to enter a marriage built on pretenses, on loving a masked version of a person. God sets the tone for holistic vulnerability, describing Adam and Eve as being "naked and unashamed" (Genesis 2:25). And while you both bring brokenness to the table, if you're in Christ, your shame has been covered. The gospel can re-create a "naked and unashamed" Christian marriage relationship.

Your past influences your personality, your emotions, your opinions, your behavior, and your convictions. And while you both have probably not attempted to conceal your background from each other, you still may not have taken the time needed to adequately examine how your past can influence your future.

For example, for most couples, marriage is a matter of two people and *two families* coming together (even more if you're beginning a stepfamily).

IF YOU HAVE BEEN MARRIED BEFORE

"Future life circumstances may release emotions that have been hibernating."
—Ron Deal, *Preparing to Blend*

Our families influence and shape us, and they need to be understood and planned for as we're preparing for marriage.

Part 1: Your Relationship History

The time you invest in this worksheet will be worth it. It'll take longer than a quick lunch break, but hey, so did touring all those potential wedding venues. Consider this a deposit of a few hours now into a fulfilling forever.

As you work through this, you'll likely uncover some gems along the way that will enrich your current relationship, but also be aware that you'll probably find some unpleasant things, too. This is normal, so don't let it discourage you.

Take your time and answer each question as thoroughly as possible. If you are going through *Preparing for Marriage* with a mentor couple, be sure to give them a copy of each of your completed worksheets.

If your upcoming marriage forms a stepfamily, this carries its own unique backstory and challenges. We suggest supplementing this study with *Preparing to Blend: The Couple's Guide to Becoming a Smart Stepfamily* by Ron Deal to fully discuss these nuances.

We're assuming your relationship is in a place of some stability to allow you to grow together and won't be rocked as you attempt to take your relationship to the next level. That said, some questions may be emotionally taxing to answer and to hear answered.

If you choose to skip a question because it's uncomfortable, anticipate the effects of avoiding—as a team of two and within yourself—what's likely a highly formative experience in your life. Notice what areas feel triggering to you (unsettling, or perhaps recalling trauma responses), and consider the very real need for counseling in some of these areas to give your relationship the strongest, most stable start possible for a bright, fulfilling future.

45

God designed marriage to be ever-growing and a safe place, allowing us to be fully known and fully loved. It can be a relationship where we give and receive glimpses of glory in how Jesus relates to us. We won't live this out perfectly, so sure, there's some risk to being vulnerable. But as we depend on God to establish a foundation of true intimacy in marriage, we can reflect Christ's love.

Need a worksheet for your partner? Find an extra one (and bonuses like help for writing your vows!) by scanning the QR code on page 159.

Your Current Relationship

1. How did we meet?

_____

_____

_____

_____

2. What attracted me to him/her?

_____

_____

_____

_____

3. How long have we been together, and how has our relationship been going?

_____

_____

_____

_____

Your Friendships

4. Friendships for me have generally been (check one):

☐ Easy—I can make friends with little to no effort.

☐ Challenging—It's a lot of work, but ultimately satisfying.

☐ So-so—I can take them or leave them.

☐ Discouraging—It's more painful than I can handle.

☐ Absent—I've never really had an authentic close friend.

☐ Other

Explain why you checked the one you did:

_____

_____

_____

_____

5. Who are two of your closest friends, and how long have they been your friends? What makes those relationships significant or special?

_____

_____

_____

_____

_____

_____

6. Which three to five words would these friends use to describe you?

_____

_____

Your Past Dating Relationships

7. Describe any serious romantic relationships from the past, if applicable. Briefly state how they began, progressed, and ended. This question is mostly about interpersonal dynamics (remember, you'll dig a little deeper into any sexual dynamics in Section Three). Acknowledge any personal contributions to unhealthy relationships, as well as ways these relationships changed you, any issues left unresolved, and any emotions you feel when reflecting on them. (Wondering how deep you should go? Consider the "love your neighbor as yourself" principle. Without prompting unnecessary curiosity, what's important for your future spouse to know?)

8. Can you identify any patterns that seem to be present in your relationships with the opposite sex? (Examples: "My tendency is to fall hard and fast, then get hurt" or "I am generally the more committed person in my relationships" or "I've always been super casual about romance.")

Part 2: Your Family

Home Environment

1. What words would you use to describe your childhood? Consider family events like vacations, significant transitions, tragedies, moves, long-held traditions, etc..

2. What was best about your childhood?

3. What was most difficult?

4. What was your family's socioeconomic, ethnic, and cultural background as you were growing up, and how did this shape your outlook on life? Did your family experience racism, abuse, trauma, or other challenges based on these demographics?

5. How would you describe the emotional environment of the home you grew up in?

....

....

....

6. Did you experience any type of abuse (physical, emotional, sexual) or other harmful relationships or relational losses in childhood or adulthood (mental illness, manipulation, addiction, codependence, etc.)? Explain as much as you are able, taking breaks as needed. If you're not ready to talk with your fiancé about this, it may be helpful to connect first with a trauma-informed counselor about your story—and to map out an intentional path to healing.

To navigate these potentially painful discussions, find these resources on FamilyLife.com:
   • "When Your Spouse Is a Survivor of Sexual Abuse" (blog post)
   • "Healing from Abuse" and "Facing Up to Abuse" (podcasts)
   • "Are You in an Abusive Relationship?" (blog post)
   • *The Wounded Heart* by Dan Allender (book)

See page 159 for a QR code with related resources.

....

....

....

....

7. What hardships (traumatic events, financial difficulties, illness, disability, affairs, death, imprisonment, separation, divorce, etc.) has your family experienced?

8. As you look back over your family history, what legacies do you see that have been passed from one generation to the next? (For example, some families might pass on a model of trusting God in tough circumstances; other families might pass on a tendency toward self-medicating to alleviate the pain of problems.)

Parents and Caregivers

Please take time to answer each of the following for all caregivers you had:

9. What words would you use to describe your parents' or caregivers' marriage—or the marriage most closely modeled for you? Explain why you chose each word.

_____

_____

_____

_____

10. As parents, what did your caregivers do well?

_____

_____

_____

_____

11. As parents or caregivers, what do you wish they would have done differently?

_____

_____

_____

_____

12. Describe the most significant impact your parents or caregivers had on you, positive or negative.

_____

_____

13. List several specific ways that each of your parents or caregivers contributed in the household.

14. In what ways did each parent show leadership in their marriage?

15. In what ways did each parent show leadership in their parenting?

16. How did they make decisions?

17. Choose three or more words to describe your relationship with your father and explain why you chose those specific words.

_____

_____

_____

_____

_____

18. Choose three or more words to describe your relationship with your mother and explain why you chose those specific words.

_____

_____

_____

_____

_____

19. In what ways are you similar to each of your parents or caregivers?

_____

_____

_____

20. In what ways are you different from each of your parents or caregivers?

_____

_____

21. Describe any unresolved issues between you and your parents or caregivers. In what ways and on what occasions do these most impact you?

22. What are your parents' or caregivers' feelings about you getting married? How do they feel about your choice of a spouse? (Tip: If their sentiment is negative toward your fiancé, don't lie about it. First, there's often a kernel of truth in even the harshest criticism. What can you privately learn and prayerfully consider from your caregiver's concern? Then, when you've sought God's wisdom and feel confident moving forward, take this opportunity to emphasize to your fiancé your commitment and your respectful, thoughtful response to your caregivers' concerns.)

Siblings and Other Relatives

23. Rate your relationship with each of your siblings (if applicable), and write a few words describing your relationship with that person:

SIBLING:	DISTANT				CLOSE
....	1	2	3	4	5
....	1	2	3	4	5
....	1	2	3	4	5
....	1	2	3	4	5
....	1	2	3	4	5
....	1	2	3	4	5

24. Describe any influential relationships you have with other relatives (grandparents, cousins, aunts, uncles, etc.) and the quantity and quality of your interactions with extended family.

....

....

....

....

....

Part 3: Your Spiritual Journey

1. What kind of religious upbringing did you have, if any?

....

....

....

....

2. What role does God play in your life today?

3. What does it mean to be a Christian, and would you describe yourself that way? If you wouldn't describe yourself that way, how would you put into words what your spiritual beliefs are?

4. How certain are you that you are in a personal relationship with the Living God?

   Absolutely certain

   Sort of certain

   Not certain at all

   Why did you answer as you did?

5. Describe your spirituality and relationship to God over the past ten years. What were the high points?

6. What were the low points?

7. What events or understanding brought more maturity and intimacy with God? What prevented that type of spiritual growth?

8. Check the areas of your life in which you find it difficult to trust and obey God:

☐ Sex
☐ Thought life
☐ Career
☐ Self-confidence
☐ Personal appearance
☐ Finances
☐ Decision-making

☐ Friendships
☐ Future
☐ Parents, stepparents, caregivers, siblings, in-laws
☐ Health
☐ Other: _____

9. On average, how often do you attend a local church? If you attend regularly, how has your involvement in a local church helped you grow in your relationship with Christ and in your commitment to following Him?

_____

_____

_____

_____

Part 4: Miscellaneous

1. Describe your patterns and any major events in handling your personal finances.

_____

_____

_____

_____

2. What are your strengths and weaknesses in handling money?

_____

_____

_____

_____

3. What type and specific amount of debt do you currently have?

_____

_____

_____

4. What types of health struggles (physical or mental) have you dealt with in the past?

5. What types of health struggles are you dealing with currently?

6. Are there ways you can proactively pursue wellness in these areas?

7. What have been your greatest successes in your work life?

8. What have been your biggest challenges in your work life?

9. What have been your greatest triumphs in life?

10. What have been your biggest disappointments in life?

11. What are the most courageous things you've ever done?

Your Life Map

Phew—your *personal history worksheet* covered a lot! It can be helpful to create a *life map* that is a more concise visual of some of the more significant events you might've just discussed together. Consider completing a life map that includes the plot points you feel have most shaped who you are today. The plot points can be positive or negative experiences, or perhaps even neutral, yet are significant to you regardless.

You can simply use the information you collected in your personal history worksheet to create a timeline with significant points or even draw a few pictures if you'd like.

You won't be able to fit your entire life story into this project, and really, that's not the point. The goal is to communicate and understand each other's personal history in general as you move closer to the day of your marriage.

Summary

We hope you found the exercises to be useful tools to look thoughtfully at your background and think through what things may be important to share with your fiancé. Again, as you review your personal history worksheets and life maps, please remember to work toward an environment of grace *and* keep in mind the principles you've already learned about authentic communication. Hear the words, but also try to discern the tone of voice and nonverbal cues. Ask clarifying and summarizing questions when appropriate, and be sure your focus as a listener is on communication and connection.

four

LET'S TALK ABOUT OUR HOPES

Our expectations constantly influence our behavior. In fact, our expectations are so intrinsic, we often don't recognize they're present even though they determine how we treat other people and how we react to situations. Most of the time, we are unaware of our expectations until they are unmet. Thinking back to Eric and Amanda in chapter 1, Eric may not realize he expected Amanda to continue watching basketball games with him until she opted to read instead. And Amanda may not realize she expected Eric to help out in the kitchen until getting home late and discovering the only thing he knows how to make them is cereal. Unmet expectations often translate to disappointments.

You'd better believe that each of us brings a certain set of expectations into a marriage. You will make particular assumptions about how you and your future spouse will live, behave, and interact with each other. The expectations can range from the routine to the deep-rooted—from dividing up household responsibilities to determining if there will be a primary breadwinner to who should initiate sex. And because both of you will have various assumptions about how your marriage will play out each day, it's critical that you explore those assumptions during your engagement so they don't lead to the poison of resentment as they periodically pop up in your marriage.

Unresolved expectations can also lead to demands, and demands can lead to manipulation. One person maneuvers the other to meet the expectation, while the other tries to avoid it. This can only lead to isolation in marriage.

The things that you hope will happen in the weeks, months, and years after the wedding ceremony might be described as your dreams for marriage. Here's the thing: dreaming about your hopes for the future doesn't have to be unrealistic. In fact, it can be quite healthy because it reveals what you value. Values include more than what we possess or desire to possess; they are much more significant than that. A value communicates, at a certain level, who you are and who you are becoming. Values tell you what you want to pursue in life and what you want to leave behind when you're gone.

Expectations without communication pretty much guarantee conflict. In the process of discussing some of the hopes, dreams, and expectations you have for your marriage, you'll discover that it's fantastic practice for learning to deal with possible differing perspectives. You won't be able to reveal every hidden expectation (some are discovered only when they're unmet, right?), but by talking them over as honestly as you can, these conversations will prevent a lot of disappointment and disillusionment.

Fantasy and Reality

What do you think of each of the following statements?

> *Our feelings of love and passion will only grow stronger after we get married.*
>
> *Life will be exciting once we're a married couple.*
>
> *Marriage will take away my feelings of loneliness.*
>
> *After we're married, my spouse will meet most of my needs.*
>
> *Once we are husband and wife, I'll be able to help my spouse become a better person.*
>
> *My marriage will very likely thrive because I'm marrying a Christian.*

While some of these statements contain a grain of truth—some larger than others—these beliefs could also lead to a mountain of disillusion-

IF YOU HAVE BEEN MARRIED BEFORE

"Routines, as well as cherished rituals and traditions, help to tell us who we are and give definition to relationships. Your new life may require that routines change, but try not to lose the meaning or connection the old routine offered."

—Ron Deal, *Preparing to Blend*

ment. Though it may be an unwelcome thought, your feelings of passion *will* tone down a bit after marriage. It's totally normal and nothing to get alarmed about—life will not always be thrilling. If marriage was constantly like that, we'd all drop dead from adrenaline overdose. It's okay when the excitement simmers down a bit; remember that you're pledging to care for each other "for better or for worse" and "in sickness and in health." Marriage is loving someone through both mirth and mundane.

Some of our expectations are based on a fantasy of romance. *This is what it's like to be in love,* culture says, and reality often plays out in sharp contrast to what we were expecting it to be like.

What other "fantasy marriage" statements are you most tempted to believe? Explain.

_____

_____

_____

_____

A Guiding Principle

As you begin to identify and discuss your hopes, values, and expectations, this portion of Scripture provides a principle for your attitudes:

> Do nothing from selfish ambition or conceit, but in humility count others more significant than yourselves. Let each of you look not only to his own interests, but also to the interests of others.
>
> Philippians 2:3–4

God's way is *always* the best way for us to happily flourish, even when our self-focused souls bristle at the idea of putting others first.

Complete the following statement: When one of my expectations is not met, I will . . .

_____

_____

_____

_____

The Christian life is ultimately *others* focused, not *me* focused. Jesus Himself lived that way (see Matthew 20:25–28). This means that our hopes and expectations, many of which are legitimate, must often be put aside for the needs of a spouse.

What I Expect from Marriage—A Survey

We've developed the following survey to help you think through a variety of expectations. Complete the survey individually. Then discuss your responses together, following these suggestions:

Try to identify where the value, hope, or expectation you hold comes from. Don't be afraid to ask yourself, *Is this a product of my background, education, culture, or personality?*

Explore the extent to which the value, hope, or expectation you hold is important to you and how you can express it in a humble and loving way.

Finally, discuss together how this value, hope, or expectation can be:

- accepted and met by your spouse
- adjusted so that it is reasonable
- abandoned as unrealistic

The survey and follow-up discussion should help you identify both realistic and unrealistic hopes, values, and expectations. The whole process is like mining for gold. You may have to move tons of earth to get ounces of gold, but those nuggets are well worth the effort it takes to find them. Many of our hopes, values, and expectations are buried beneath a lifetime of conditioning, so it takes work to uncover them.

As you write down specific expectations, values, and hopes you have for your marriage in the following categories, be sure to write how *you* feel about the particular topic, not what you think your fiancé wants to hear. The more specific and honest you are, the more you'll discover.

You can download a copy of the survey by scanning the QR code on page 159.

Are you forming a stepfamily with this marriage? Once again, because we can only briefly address those complexities here, we suggest adding to this study with *Preparing to Blend: The Couple's Guide to Becoming a Smart Stepfamily* by Ron Deal.

Marriage Relationship

1. How will we make decisions once we are married, and what will we do if we can't agree?

2. How will we work through and resolve conflict? How do I expect to be approached when my spouse wants to bring an issue to me?

3. How often do I expect to spend time with my friends after we are married?

4. How will I relate to opposite-sex friends after we are married? If I have an ex-spouse, what do we consider wise boundaries about how you and I will each relate to them?

Finances

5. What are my thoughts about our current salaries? Are we okay with one or the other being the primary provider of our financial resources, and if so, which one? Why?

6. In what ways do we hope to mutually support each other in pursuing careers?

7. How will we decide on major purchases? In general, what constitutes "major"?

8. Who will pay the bills and keep track of expenses?

9. Will we share money and bank accounts or keep separate accounts, credit cards, funds, etc.? Do we see it as *our* money or more *mine* and *theirs*?

10. What is my philosophy of giving (to charitable donations, to the Church, or to other organizations or ministries)? How will we make decisions about giving?

11. What are my guiding principles about debt and credit cards?

Home

12. Where do I want us to live? What are key influencing factors and underlying values about where I choose to live?

13. In what setting would I prefer to live (city, suburb, small town, rural, etc.)?

14. Do I want us to live in an apartment or house? Will we rent or buy?

15. How soon after we are married do I expect to have our home reasonably furnished?

16. What do I expect our standard of living to look like after five years of marriage? Ten years? Twenty years?

Social/Entertainment/Home Environment

17. How important to me are mealtimes as a couple, with our immediate family, or with extended family? What do I hope those look like, and why? How often will we eat out?

18. Do I want a pet in our home? If so, what type?

19. How often do I want to invite people over to our home?

20. What kind of entertaining do I expect to do (formal or informal dinners, large or cozy gatherings, casual hangouts, etc.)?

21. How often do I want us to go out on dates with each other?

22. What changes, if any, do I expect our marriage to have on existing friendships with others?

23. What hobbies or recreational activities do I want to pursue individually and together?

24. How much time do I hope to give to hobbies and recreational activities—both on my own and those we do together?

25. How do I feel about drinking alcohol or having alcoholic beverages in our home? What about smoking, vaping, and marijuana?

Media Consumption

26. What will be the role of screen time in our home, and what guidelines should we have about what we will watch?

27. What boundaries will we put in place around screen time, mobile devices in bed, time on phones, etc.?

28. Will we share our social media accounts and passwords with each other? Why or why not?

29. What role will gaming play in our home? What guidelines and boundaries will we have around this?

30. What should be our guidelines about watching content made for "mature audiences"?

Household Responsibilities

31. How will we share meal-prep responsibilities, and how will we decide what types of food we will eat (vegan, organic, low carb)?

_____

_____

_____

_____

_____

32. What are some guidelines you typically live by as a single person for the cleanliness and order of your home? How are they the same or different from your fiancé?

_____

_____

_____

_____

_____

33. How will we divide up these household tasks?

Laundry _____

Buying groceries _____

Car maintenance _____

Home repairs and yard work _____

General household cleaning _____

Making the bed _____

Meal prep: cooking and cleanup _____

Children and Parenting

34. In general, how do I feel about having kids of our own?

35. If one or both of us brings kids into the marriage, what role do I picture the nonbiological parent playing? How would I describe my relationship with each child right now, biological or not?

36. When would I like us to start having kids of our own, and how many do I want to have? What would we do if we cannot conceive biological children? Is adoption an option for us?

37. What is my view on birth control?

38. What is my view on abortion? (Someday you might face all of these things in your own body and marriage, or you may have encountered them already. It's better to talk openly now than have these issues ambush you. If you've experienced an abortion or chosen this with a previous partner, consider talking about this significant experience with your fiancé. Because this could be a very difficult conversation, we recommend inviting the help of a counselor into the discussion.)

_____

_____

_____

_____

39. Which, if either, of us do we see potentially staying home to care for our kids? How do we see ourselves potentially dividing the responsibilities of raising them and training them to love God and others?

_____

_____

_____

_____

40. How do I envision that we would share the responsibility of disciplining our children, and how will that discipline play out? Are there any types of discipline I know I want to avoid?

_____

_____

_____

_____

Spiritual

41. When and how often will we pray together and discuss the Bible and what God is doing in our lives?

42. To what extent and in what ways will we be involved with a local community of dedicated, active Christians?

43. In what ways do I anticipate communicating our faith with others as a couple?

44. How will we both continue to grow spiritually, and what will spiritual leadership look like in our home?

Holidays/Vacations/Special Occasions

45. Where and with whom will we spend major holidays?

46. How will we decide?

47. What expectations do I have for major holidays? What specific holidays, values, and traditions feel important to me?

48. How often will we go on vacation, and what are my desires for what a vacation will look like?

49. How will we celebrate birthdays and wedding anniversaries?

50. How much will we spend on gifts for family, friends, and each other (birthdays, Christmas, weddings, anniversaries, etc.)?

51. What do I want a typical weekend to involve? Do I want to observe Sabbath as a family? What might that look like? (Sabbath, the fourth commandment, is essentially the practice of ceasing from work to rest. It both reminds us that we are limited beings who need rest and that God is an infinite being who holds the world—and us—together.)

Parents, Caregivers, and Other Relatives

52. How do I think our relationships with our parents or caregivers will change after we're married?

53. How much time do I anticipate spending with my parents or care-givers, extended family, and in-laws?

54. What other relatives (siblings, cousins, grandparents, etc.) do I expect to be involved with? In what ways will we be involved with them?

55. How involved do I want my parents or caregivers, extended family, and in-laws to be in our children's lives? How will we accomplish this?

56. How will we handle caring for our aging parents later in life if that is needed? To what lengths are we willing to go for this?

Sex

Note, we will discuss some very sensitive topics in great depth. Depending on your individual responses and individual sexual histories, these conversations would potentially need to be supported by the help of a mentor couple or counselor.

57. Do you expect sex to be challenging or easy or somewhere in between? Elaborate on your response.

_____

_____

_____

_____

58. What is my past experience with pornography? Is this a current struggle? (It's likely that you or your fiancé may have already encountered challenges around pornography. As above, while it might be difficult to discuss, it's far better to talk openly now.) What steps will we take as a couple to protect ourselves and our relationship from porn?

_____

_____

_____

_____

59. What are my expectations about sex on our honeymoon?

_____

_____

_____

_____

60. In our first year of marriage, how often do I expect us to have sex? Who do I expect to initiate?

_____

_____

_____

_____

61. How will we handle it if/when the sexual aspect of our relationship doesn't go well? What if one of us is unable to have sex for a short time or a longer season? How do we expect the other to respond?

_____

_____

_____

62. What do I feel about my spouse sometimes saying *no* to having sex?

_____

_____

_____

63. How do we plan to keep our sexual intimacy a priority throughout the span of our marriage?

_____

_____

_____

Summary

You guys are putting so much thought and energy into preparing well for your marriage—way to go! If you've uncovered any expectations your fiancé holds that don't feel resolved or resolvable to you, it is worth spending a bit more time individually searching your hearts and seeking God's wisdom. It could also be important to seek wisdom from a godly friend or mentor if anything is giving you major pause or alarm. Keep your communication open.

five

LET'S LISTEN TO OUR PEOPLE

One thing I'm increasingly convinced of the older I get: Life is best experienced in the context of community. As we saw in chapter 1, God made us to be social beings who enjoy intimacy and unity with others, so when we separate ourselves or break away from others, things will not go well for us. Without positive and reliable input from a trusted community around us, poor decision-making and distorted thought processes can easily gain a foothold and influence us in unhealthy ways. Conversely, if we proactively involve other caring Christians in our lives, they are often able to spot areas where we might be prone to compromise, to endanger our character, and even to damage our marriage. As Proverbs 11:14 says, "Where there is no guidance, a people falls, but in an abundance of counselors there is safety."

For engaged couples, the struggle is real with the temptation to isolate yourselves and to neglect, or even cut out, others in your lives. *We've got so much planning to do*, a couple might say, or *We just want time for the two of us.*

But as true as both of these statements might be (depending on your specific engagement relationship), it's never a good idea to allow consistent seclusion as a pair during this unique season. Distancing yourself from important friends or family members can lead to an unhealthy obsession with your fiancé, waning interest in the world beyond him or her, and diminished healthy communication.

If saying *yes* to your fiancé means always saying *no* to your other friends and family, this is a concern that needs to be addressed sooner rather than later. You need godly people in your life both as individuals and as a couple to give you balance and perspective. You need input from friends and family who have insights that you don't. And the people around you need you, too! You need people in your life. If you want your relationship to be healthy—now and in the future—you cannot disengage from others.

We're not saying that your relationship should be everyone's business to the point that too many people are giving you advice on every tiny detail. However, we are saying that you should involve the people you trust the most. Wise people who know you and who make godly contributions to your life. People like your parents or caregivers, a mentor couple, Bible study leaders, or a pastor or pastoral counselor—individuals who will ask you the tough questions about good decision-making, maintaining sexual integrity, and the spiritual health of your relationship.

Without listening to and inviting healthy involvement from others, false messages and our own selfishness can quickly creep in and deteriorate godly relationships.

A couple in isolation is a couple in danger, so surround yourselves with godly men and women who care about you and love Christ. If you do, you'll be laying the right kind of foundation, bringing honor to the Lord now as you are engaged and in the future when you are married.

The Wisdom of Parents and Caregivers—A Questionnaire

Hopefully we've helped you see the wisdom of inviting others you trust to speak into your coming marriage. Naturally, you might be wondering how to go about intentionally receiving help. Good news: These next two exercises will give you some tracks to run on in pursuing godly marital advisers.

The first project seeks to help you gain understanding about yourself and your fiancé via the lens of each other's parents, caregivers, or stepparents. It's designed to help you accomplish two distinct things.

First, it will help you honor your parents or caregivers by seeking their advice and counsel (see Proverbs 6:20). The process of asking your parents or caregivers these questions also offers the insight of those who know you best . . . or *at least* the longest.

Second, this process will help you honor your future in-laws by involving them in the process of helping you understand how to love their child. I have been personally blessed by discovering that your relationship with your in-laws can be one of the richest in your life. Honoring them at the start of your marriage is a wise step that could really benefit everyone involved.

Before we go further, an important caveat: We understand that lots of us come from difficult family backgrounds. The destructive consequences of alcoholism, abuse, neglect, mental illness, or alienation follow many people into marriage. If any of these, or something in a similar vein, are part of your situation with your parents or caregivers, you may decide it isn't appropriate to complete this project with them. This is okay; don't force it just because it's included in this book.

Still, we'd like to encourage you to find someone you trust who can speak into your relationship. It might not be your or your fiancé's family of origin, but you do need to have input from someone you trust who is farther down life's journey than you. Is there a mentor, Sunday school teacher, former coach, aunt, or uncle who could help with this section?

Options and Instructions

Here are three options for completing this exercise; choose the one you feel best fits your situation.

Option A: Send a copy of the questionnaire to your parents or caregivers and future in-laws along with a few words of instruction explaining the project. Ask them to get their answers back to you within one or two weeks.

Option B: Set aside a time when you can give your parents or caregivers and future in-laws a call to go through the questionnaire with them. You'll probably want to send them the questions beforehand so they can think about and discuss their answers in advance.

Option C: Arrange to have a meal or coffee with your parents or caregivers to go over the questionnaire with them. As with Option B, let them know the questions beforehand so they can think about their answers. Ask your parents or caregivers their questions first, then your fiancé can ask the in-law questions second.

If your parents or caregivers or in-laws are divorced, talk with your fiancé about the best way to proceed. Remember, you may want to ask these questions of stepparents if you have a strong relationship, or you may want to only ask your biological parents or caregivers. Generally speaking, the more parents or caregivers who are involved, the better. However, you must decide what is appropriate and best for you at this time.

Feel free to adapt the questionnaire if you sense that certain questions may be difficult or awkward for a parent to answer.

You can download a copy of the questionnaire by scanning the QR code on page 159.

Questionnaire

For parents or caregivers: Please answer the following questions as if your child were asking them. If you are unable to answer a question, feel free to move on to the next one.

1. What *strengths* do you see in my life that will help me in marriage?

_____

_____

_____

_____

2. What *weaknesses* do you see in my life that will be a challenge for me to work on and overcome in my marriage?

_____

_____

_____

_____

3. If you could give me one piece of advice about marriage (based on what you did right or wrong), what would it be and why?

4. What is your best advice to me in the following areas as I move into my marriage relationship? (Choose three to five of the following prompts to comment on.)

Finances:

Communication:

Sex:

Husband/Wife Roles:

Commitment/Faithfulness:

Fun and Leisure:

Being a Parent:

Spiritual Growth:

_____

_____

Priorities in Life:

_____

_____

_____

_____

Work:

_____

_____

_____

_____

5. If you could keep just one memory or experience from all your married life, what would it be and why?

_____

_____

_____

_____

6. Is there anything special or meaningful to you that you would like us to consider including in the wedding ceremony?

_____

_____

_____

7. How do you anticipate my relationship with you, as my parents or caregivers, will change now that I am marrying and starting a new family?

_____

_____

_____

_____

8. How do you expect we'll handle holidays after we get married?

_____

_____

_____

_____

9. Would you like it if we dropped in unannounced, or would you prefer that we contact you before visiting?

_____

_____

_____

_____

10. Do you have any specific hopes about where we will live? Attend church?

_____

_____

_____

_____

For future in-laws: Answer these questions as if your future son-in-law or daughter-in-law were asking them to you.

1. What are some qualities you see in me, or know about me, that make me a helpful life partner to your son/daughter?

2. What personal advice would you give me about your son/daughter that will help me be the life partner he/she needs?

3. What would you like me to call you after we are married?

The Wisdom of Mentor Couples—An Interview

Learning from couples ahead of you—who've been there, done that—can be a rewarding and beneficial experience for your engagement and future marriage. This interview with a mentor couple will help you discover what seeds you need to be planting now to have a vibrant marriage.

Instructions

Complete this interview with your mentor couple or with a couple that has been married at least five years whose relationship both of you respect and admire. If you choose someone besides your mentors, ask the couple in mind if they would spend some time with you to complete a simple, zero-prep nine-question interview about marriage and family life that is part of your premarital preparation.

Do the interview over a meal, dessert, or coffee. You may want to take turns asking the questions. If you have other questions you'd like to ask them, go for it. Take advantage of time with a couple that's a bit farther down the path. Be sure to ask clarifying and summary questions if you aren't clear on something they say.

Take notes on their answers. You'll probably find that the insights you hear in this interview will be words you want to refer to later.

Interview Questions

Looking Back

1. Describe how you met and got engaged. What attracted you to each other? How did you propose? What were some of the emotions you felt in the time between your engagement and your wedding?

2. What are some of your fondest memories of the first years of your marriage? Why?

3. What were the greatest areas of conflict or tension in your first few years of marriage? How did you handle them?

4. How has your relationship with God affected your relationship with each other?

Looking at the Present

5. What have you learned about your spouse that has been most helpful to you as you seek to understand and love each other?

6. What are the greatest areas of conflict in your marriage today? What spiritual principles have been most helpful to you in solving these tensions?

7. How do you manage schedules, work demands, and outside activities while maintaining family as a priority?

8. What are some practical ways you have found to keep your relationship with God a priority in your marriage and family?

Looking Ahead

9. What advice would you give us that you think will make the greatest difference in our marriage twenty years from now?

section three

WHERE WE'RE GOING

Now that we've set a solid foundation for marriage—and dug into a lot of where you both are right now in terms of your pasts and your expectations—it's time to have some good conversations about where you want your marriage to go and how to get there. In Section Three, we're going to have conversations about how you want to approach a few of the main areas you'll navigate in your relationship.

As with the previous sections, before talking together, work through each conversation on your own, giving yourself plenty of time to think through your answers. Record your responses in the space provided after each question, and then come together to discuss them.

If you are going through *Preparing for Marriage* with a marriage mentor or mentor couple, you have the choice of either discussing your answers as a couple before you meet with your mentor(s) or discussing your answers for the first time when you meet with your mentor(s).

six

LET'S TALK ABOUT MONEY

If you want to test a couple's sense of unity, look at how they handle their finances. It may be the most important test any couple faces as husband and wife.

Statistically, couples list finances as one of the leading causes of conflict in their marriage. Oddly enough, it's usually not the lack of money that causes problems; it's how they handle what they have and how they communicate about it.

How someone manages their money reveals much about their character, desires, priorities, and even their relationship with God. Put two people together in marriage, and you can see that financial conversations are really conversations about deeply held values.

This is not a one-and-done discussion. Married couples can work most of their lives at communicating with each other about financial issues and still be in process. Decisions on spending, saving, giving, investing, hobbies, allowances, and many other related issues are all worked out over the years. Yet you can still save yourselves a great deal of conflict after you get married if you engage in a few key discussions now.

Backgrounds

There's no one way that people approach money, and we tend to mimic what we learned as we grew up. Our backgrounds often determine our attitudes and methods.

For example, some of us have parents or caregivers who are more spontaneous spenders, and that has rubbed off on us. If we walk into a store and see something we'd like to purchase, we usually get it. Others of us, however, were raised in an environment where our caregivers were extremely careful about spending and much more interested in saving and investing. As you might expect, this can lead to a lot of heated conversations. But if you're committed to each other and to seeking God's purposes for your family, you can make it work.

Money is a tool that carries potential for both purpose and peril, so you must decide how you will manage it *together*. Ask yourselves, *How can we use it without loving it or allowing it to use us?* Starting out cautiously will put you both on better footing than starting out with little or no restraint.

1. How would you describe your general attitude about money—saving, spending, budgeting, giving, etc.?

2. What mistakes have you made where money is concerned?

3. Make a list of the possible financial mistakes you could most likely make in your first years of marriage. These can be attitudes, actions, or beliefs.

Financial mistakes are all too common for married couples. Many people become adults with little-to-no training on how to handle money. They don't know how to set priorities, they're influenced by the culture or their peers, and they lack the basic discipline needed to set and keep a budget. Most importantly, they lack God's perspective on wise handling of finances.

When it comes to money, a biblical foundation is built on two key principles:

All of our resources belong to God.

We are the managers of His resources.

Without setting out together to build your life on these rock-solid principles instead of any other financial advice or marketing messages, you'll be susceptible to all kinds of financial sinkholes—decisions based on fear, greed, impulse, materialism, and false priorities.

Who Does Our Money Really Belong To?

4. Read the following passages and circle the phrases in these verses that indicate ownership.

> *The earth is the Lord's and the fullness thereof, the world and those who dwell therein.*
>
> *Psalm 24:1*

> *Yours, O Lord, is the greatness and the power and the glory and the victory and the majesty, for all that is in the heavens and in the earth is yours. Yours is the kingdom, O Lord, and you are exalted as head above all. Both riches and honor come from you, and you rule over all. In your hand are power and might, and in your hand it is to make great and to give strength to all. . . . For all things come from you, and of your own have we given you. . . . O Lord our God, all this abundance that we have provided for building*

101

you a house for your holy name comes from your hand and is all your own.

1 Chronicles 29:11–12, 14, 16

5. How should the truth that God owns everything affect the way you view material possessions and financial resources? Give a specific example of how you could apply this in your coming marriage.

_____

_____

_____

_____

6. Explain your thoughts about the following statement: "I'll give God ten percent of my income and spend the other ninety percent however I want."

_____

_____

_____

It's natural to feel that what we earn is ours, but the Bible makes it clear that God actually owns it all. Everything belongs to Him, and we are managers of what He has placed in our care.

If God Is the Owner, What Does That Make Us?

7. What does the following passage say about our responsibility for the resources God has given us?

One who is faithful in a very little is also faithful in much, and one who is dishonest in a very little is also dishonest in much. If then you have not been faithful in the unrighteous wealth, who will entrust to you the true riches? And if you have not been faithful in that which is another's, who will give you that which is your own? No servant can serve two masters, for either he will hate the one and love the other, or he will be devoted to the one and despise the other. You cannot serve God and money.

Luke 16:10–13

_____

_____

_____

_____

8. The second foundational truth regarding finances flows from the first. If God owns it all, then we are not owners but managers of His resources. What are the choices of a manager according to the passage you just read from Luke?

_____

_____

_____

_____

A manager is a person who manages property, finances, or affairs on behalf of the owner. A manager acts as a supervisor or administrator. God entrusts us to manage His resources for His specific goals in our lives and in the lives of others.

9. The passage from Luke offers yet another foundational truth regarding finances: You cannot serve both God and money. What additional insight does the following passage add?

Do not lay up for yourselves treasures on earth, where moth and rust destroy and where thieves break in and steal, but lay up for yourselves treasures in heaven, where neither moth nor rust destroys and where thieves do not break in and steal. For where your treasure is, there your heart will be also.

Matthew 6:19–21

10. What ultimately happens when people try to store up treasures on earth rather than in heaven? Can you think of an example of someone you know or have heard about who did so?

God not only owns it all, but He is also the one who supplies our needs. Read this passage and then answer the following questions.

Therefore I tell you, do not be anxious about your life, what you will eat or what you will drink, nor about your body, what you will put on. Is not life more than food, and the body more than clothing? Look at the birds of the air: they neither sow nor reap nor gather into barns, and yet your heavenly Father feeds them. Are you not of more value than they? And which of you by being anxious can add a single hour to his span of life? And why are you anxious about clothing? Consider the lilies of the field, how they grow: they neither toil nor spin, yet I tell you, even Solomon in all his glory was not arrayed like one of these. But if God so clothes the grass of the field, which today is alive and tomorrow is thrown into the oven, will he not much more clothe you, O you of little faith? Therefore do not be anxious, saying, "What shall we eat?" or "What shall we drink?" or "What shall we wear?" For the Gentiles seek after all these things, and your heavenly Father knows that you need them all. But seek first the kingdom of God and his righteousness, and all these things will be added to you.

Matthew 6:25–33

11. Do you find it easy or difficult to turn your money-related anxieties over to God? Why?

12. Do you find it easy or difficult to live within your means—to live according to what God has provided—without going into debt? In what particular areas are you most likely to overspend, if you do (clothing, entertainment, travel, gifts, etc.)? What is the value most likely compelling your overspending? (This could be approval of others, a sense of security, compensating for a sense of guilt or fear, etc.)

Spiritual Decisions

Because we are managers of the resources God has entrusted to us, every financial decision we make is actually a spiritual decision. Each one speaks to our trust, wisdom, generosity, and the health of our emotions. That may sound revolutionary (or, to some, ridiculous), but how we manage finances is a pretty good indicator of the condition of our spiritual life.

13. How do you think you might apply the principles you've learned so far to each of the following areas?

Forming, maintaining, and living within a budget:

_____

_____

_____

_____

The lifestyle you will lead as a married couple:

_____

_____

_____

_____

Giving:

_____

_____

_____

_____

Debt:

_____

_____

_____

_____

Even though it's countercultural, knowing God's perspective on finances profoundly influences money management. You might realize, for example, that you have a responsibility to live within the means God has given you. You'll look more closely at your attitudes about material possessions and give more thought to spending and purchasing. You'll also want to give more generously toward the work of God through your church, etc.

In the context of these truths—that God owns it all and we are managers of His resources—decide how you will approach money issues together. In developing a biblical view of finances as a team, you will experience one of the great privileges and joys of marriage.

It's worth saying again: How you handle money in your marriage may be the biggest test of your relationship. Now, before you get married, is the best time to commit to oneness in your finances. This means:

- Viewing money as *ours* rather than *mine*
- Being open and honest about finances and not keeping secrets about income, spending, assets, debt, etc.
- Forming a budget together and working alongside each other to stick to it
- Making important financial decisions together
- Setting financial goals together

Tip: If one of these feels tough, spend time together, alone, or with a trusted friend determining why this is hard. Money amplifies what's at our core, revealing ways we do or don't trust a partner, ways we might not feel valued, our own fears, or what we long to protect. As you determine the truth, get honest with your fiancé.

IF YOUR MARRIAGE WILL START A BLENDED FAMILY

"Merging money and merging family relationships are always tied together in blended families."

—Ron Deal, *Preparing to Blend*

Financial issues can either divide or unite. Working together to manage what God has entrusted to you can make you stronger teammates full of shared responsibility and generous purpose.

Most couples find that they differ quite a bit in a number of areas related to finances. Remember, however, that your differences can work in a way that bonds you together. As Christians, we function like a body does: "If all were a single member, where would the body be?" (1 Corinthians 12:19). You need each other's values, capacities, backgrounds, and skills for the wisest, most holistic management possible.

14. Individually, make a list of five to seven material possessions that you highly value. Be specific (my car, my furniture, etc.), and then share your lists with each other. This will help you gain insight about each other as you head into marriage.

_____

_____

_____

_____

15. What are some financial goals or dreams you would like to pursue in order to manage resources well and further God's purposes in the world?

_____

_____

_____

_____

seven

LET'S TALK ABOUT SEX

It's Time to Have "The Talk" Again

Whether your parents had "the talk" with you when you were young, you learned about sex from kids who had no more knowledge about it than you did, or you were left to wonder and wander on your own, it's time for "the talk" again. Only this time you have a truer picture of what's at stake, and there is now a person in your life who deserves—and needs—your love and your respect.

God designed sex to be a deeply caring, mutual, enjoyable experience—in a healthy marriage relationship. Though people may balk at the Bible's sexual values and stamp them "expired," God teaches us to love in life-giving ways, and that includes the way you love each other sexually as husband and wife. When sex is approached selfishly, if you treat your partner as only a means for your gratification, that's essentially *using*—not loving. God's ways are the path to the healthiest, most healing, and most fulfilling sex possible.

The Boundaries Are Good

I get that it can be confusing: Sex before you're married can *feel* holy and good. I've heard the honest question before: "How can this be wrong?!"

God created sex and He created it to be *awe*some. It's not surprising that it can feel like a taste of heaven—even outside of marriage.

Sexual integrity is about surrendering our desires to God—before and throughout the duration of marriage. In obedience and trust, we set loving boundaries and practice self-control for our good and the good of others. First Thessalonians affirms this higher view of sex: "It is God's will that you should be sanctified: that you should avoid sexual immorality; that each of you should learn to control your own body in a way that is holy and honorable, not in passionate lust like the pagans, who do not know God; and that in this matter *no one should wrong or take advantage of a brother or sister*" (4:3–6 NIV, emphasis added).

Think of the metaphor in this proverb: "Can a man carry fire next to his chest and his clothes not be burned?" (Proverbs 6:27). Fire is beautiful, warming, comforting, and inviting. But take it from the proper environment (like a fireplace or fire pit), and fire is damaging and destructive. Sex is a stunning gift within the environment of a marriage relationship, but outside of that context, it can be devastating. God knows this, and because He loves you and wants you to experience the joys of intimacy, He has created the safe boundaries of marriage. His boundaries are intended to protect you from the harm of things like:

adultery

sexually transmitted disease

porn addiction

lack of sexual desire (due to guilt) once you're married

comparing your spouse to fantasies or previous sexual partners

improper expectations of your spouse because of previous sexual experiences or fantasies

trying to use sex to fix problems or end arguments

being selfish, demanding, or even abusive in the bedroom

wrapping your identity around your sexual performance or desirability

Note: We certainly recognize that some have been deeply impacted by trauma in this area. One in five women, for example, will experience sexual violence in their lifetime, almost half from an acquaintance. And

IF YOU'RE CONCERNED ABOUT YOUR PAST . . .

If you have a sexual history that you are reluctant to talk about, we encourage you to read the section on page 117, "Sharing Your Sexual History with Your Fiancé." This will offer some guidelines on the appropriate level of disclosure regarding your sexual experience.

the number is almost the same for men: one in six experience some form of sexual abuse. A healthy marriage can act as a place of deep healing . . . safe, tender, and mutual interactions can nurture the difficult process of healing from the inside out. But sometimes, pursuing married sex without addressing deeply rooted emotional pain can create more harm. Could one of you use counseling to address previous sexual pain? You will be rewriting narratives of brokenness and theft with wholeness.

What Is Sex for Then?

Sex is not merely a physical act. God created it as a process of intimate communication affecting our souls and emotions, of which the physical act of sex is a significant part. It's a powerful, emotional bonding experience designed to strengthen a marriage.

God wants us to experience the absolute best rather than a cheapened version of the real thing. In light of that, for each of the following verses, state in your own words the purpose you see that God has for sex in marriage.

> *Let your fountain be blessed, and rejoice in the wife of your youth,*
> *a lovely deer, a graceful doe. Let her breasts fill you at all times*
> *with delight; be intoxicated always in her love.*
>
> *Proverbs 5:18–19*

1. According to this verse, one purpose God has for sex is:

_____

_____

*God blessed them [Adam and Eve]; and God said to them, "Be
fruitful and multiply, and fill the earth. . . ."*

Genesis 1:28 NASB

*Behold, children are a gift of the Lord, the fruit of the womb is a
reward. Like arrows in the hand of a warrior, so are the children
of one's youth. Blessed is the man whose quiver is full of them.*

Psalm 127:3–5 NASB

2. According to these verses, another purpose God has for sex is:

_____

_____

*"The two shall become one flesh." So they are no longer two but
one flesh. What therefore God has joined together, let not man
separate.*

Mark 10:8–9

My beloved is mine, and I am his.
Song of Solomon 2:16

3. According to these verses, a third purpose God has for sex in
   marriage is:

_____

_____

4. How does this biblical picture of sex affect your view of it? Are
   you surprised at all by what the Bible teaches? If so, why?

_____

_____

_____

_____

5. What, if anything, seems difficult for you to accept about these purposes for sex found in the Scripture references above? Why?

_____

_____

_____

_____

Sex is for:

- Pleasure: Sex is intended for the pleasure and enjoyment of a man and woman who are married. It's also important to know that in marriage, pleasure given is pleasure received; serving your spouse with this unique and enjoyable gift honors God and deepens your love for each other.

- Growing families: Sex is intended to quite literally create the next generation. And like we said before, healthy, godly marriages are greenhouses for passing on a strong faith to the next generation.

- Strengthening of the marriage relationship: Think of it this way. If you're so busy enjoying each other, you won't have the time or desire to look for enjoyment elsewhere. Set your mind to that level of committed enjoyment of your spouse. What we absolutely do not mean is that if your marriage has a season of little to no sex you are justified in looking for your "needs" to be met outside your marriage. Each person is responsible to his or her vows of sexual integrity, regardless of your spouse's sexual output. Sometimes sex isn't possible or wise for a season. Still, pursuing regular, mutually fulfilling and satisfying intimacy within your marriage will increase the fun, pleasure, and deepening bond between you and your spouse. The giving of yourself to your spouse sexually is an expression—even a declaration and celebration—of the bond God has fashioned between the two of you.

An Incredible Gift

In the context of a satisfying marriage relationship, sex serves as a holy bond. It is the most personal and private act a husband and wife can share, and it acts as a celebration of their unity and oneness.

Because this bond is so sacred and powerful, breaking it through infidelity can cause devastation to a marriage. It's critical for you and your spouse to do what you can to protect your relationship once you're married. After all, it's the protection of a gift given to you by a loving and perfectly wise God.

It's worth saying again: Does this mean a spouse is responsible for their partner's infidelity or porn? Absolutely not. When sex becomes an obligation—particularly out of fear—that's an issue that can cause lasting pain. Both must be committed to faithfulness and to responding to and receiving your spouse through every season life holds.

Sex in marriage is the physical expression of what is true about a couple on the emotional, mental, and spiritual levels. It is the gift God has given to a husband and wife to communicate love and to demonstrate emotional and spiritual unity on a physical plane.

Understanding Your Differences

Researchers continue to observe differences in the attitudes, needs, and responses we each bring into a sexual relationship. Every person is unique, but there are still some differences that can be related to our gender—like whether our sexual response is slow and distractable (as many women experience) or fast and focused (as men statistically tend toward). But none of us like being on the receiving end of stereotypes. The moment generalizations stop creating authentic understanding, they stop being helpful.

Suffice it to say, you and your spouse will have some differences in how you approach sex and intimacy. Sex isn't formulaic.

Like money, sex is influenced by our personalities and backstories and schedule and relational conflict and everything else. Sexual desire will ebb and flow with your hormones, diet, exercise, soundproofing of your bedroom door, and whether your boss belittled you at work that day.

The following questions are meant to create thoughtful dialogue with your fiancé. Seek how you can understand your fiancé's story in advance, and also how to communicate your own background to be understood. Take time to answer the next three questions on your own before discussing with your fiancé.

6. What sexual differences do you anticipate based on what you already know about influencing factors between you? Consider what you've discussed with family-of-origin dynamics, past sexual relationships, etc. Also consider how you have been taught or modeled what each gender "is supposed to do" or messages about your body you may have internalized. Discuss how these influence you and your potential response to sexual intimacy. How can you address these differences in a healthy way?

7. How can you continue to lovingly communicate differences as they arise, respect each other's differences, and consider how to make sexual encounters intimate and enjoyable for you both?

8. How can you learn to recognize each other's sexual desires and to communicate your physical and emotional needs?

_____

_____

_____

_____

Anticipations and Anxieties

Complete the following individually and then share your answers with each other.

9. Individually, write down three or four things you are eagerly anticipating in your sexual relationship and three or four things you are anxious about.

Anticipation:

_____

_____

_____

_____

Anxiety:

_____

_____

_____

10. Is there anything else you'd like your fiancé to understand about you in the realm of sexuality?

_____

_____

_____

_____

Now share your answers with each other, and ask your fiancé what you can do now, or later, to address the most pressing anxiety issue. Also discuss any differing expectations that may have come up.

11. What are the most important insights you have gained from this chapter about God's design for sexual intimacy?

_____

_____

_____

_____

Sharing Your Sexual History with Your Fiancé

Note: Again, at this intimate level, trauma and destructive decisions of others and ourselves do change us, often affecting every aspect of us. But a trustworthy, loving marriage can offer safe opportunities to reimagine and redeem sex as God designed it to be. Safe interactions addressing the whole person can nurture this difficult healing process from the inside out.

Yet without addressing deeply rooted emotional pain, even married sex can aggravate harm. Consider whether trauma counseling could be necessary to pave the way for a lifetime of connected, fulfilling sex.

As you prepare for marriage, maybe you've had hardly any sexual experience. You've committed to only having sex with your spouse, and you may feel some anxiety about inexperience or the unknowns to come in you and your soon-to-be spouse's relationship. Maybe you are on the other side of that, looking back with regret at sexual choices you've made in the past. You may also wonder, *How much of the past do I need to share with my fiancé?* And truthfully, even if the whole of both of your sexual experiences is confined to your relationship together, since it's outside of a marriage that's yet to come, that affects your relationship, too.

This is not an easy conversation no matter where you find yourself, for several reasons:

- Sharing your past mistakes and sins may lead to several painful days between you as a couple.
- It may mean reliving incidents you'd rather forget.
- There might even be the fear of a broken engagement.

You may be tempted to avoid sharing anything from your past. This includes sexual behaviors as well as any sexual abuse you have faced.

Christ is eager to heal our hurt and forgive any damaging decisions. The Bible says, "There is therefore now no condemnation for those who are in Christ Jesus" (Romans 8:1). We see His compassion extended to the woman caught in adultery, whose life He saves and who He forgives: "Neither do I condemn you; go, and from now on sin no more" (John 8:11).

And while these things are absolutely true in our relationship with God, there can be consequences of past sins—those you've committed or those that have been committed against you—that need to be honestly grappled with as you move toward marriage. While you do not need to share every detail, you cannot avoid the fact that your life has been shaped by these things. If you and your fiancé desire to approach marriage on a firm footing, you need to be honest with each other and deal with your pasts. It is better to speak the truth prior to your marriage than to live with the fear, deceit, and shame that come from hiding the truth from your spouse.

There is one other benefit to sharing your past. True healing can occur when you confess your sins to each other (James 5:16). God has used marriage to heal individuals from past hurts that have haunted them for years. This is especially true when dealing with sexual sin. Many men and women have found forgiveness, mercy, and liberty from shame by confessing these scarring circumstances to their future spouses. As in many aspects of marriage, God can use a spouse (or future spouse) to be a tangible expression of the gospel.

Of course, these are not easy issues to discuss. And keep in mind there is no cookie-cutter solution to what you may be facing. But in an effort to guide those who are struggling with knowing what to do and how to go about it, here are some principles and perspectives.

1. Make a list of all that you are feeling a need to share with him or her. Note, however, this is not a time for great detail—just a list of events, choices, or hurts you've experienced. This list may contain things you've done that you now regret or things that have happened to you.

2. Once you've completed your list, make sure you have experienced God's forgiveness, cleansing, and healing for everything you've written. If you haven't yet done so, spend some time in prayer, repenting of and confessing any sin. Remember, God tells us in 1 John 1:9, "If we confess our sins, he is faithful and just to forgive us our sins and to cleanse us from all unrighteousness."

3. Determine which items on your list you should discuss with your fiancé and why. If you have doubts about any items, make sure you seek wise and godly counsel before talking with your fiancé. Another person's compassionate, listening ear and prayerful concern can guide you before and after you marry.

4. Set a time and place to talk with your fiancé. Choose a private setting where you are both free to express your emotions. Choose a time when you will both be refreshed and have capacity to talk about heavy subjects. Tiredness can trigger unhealthy emotions and reactions.

5. Before you meet, pray that your fiancé will have the strength and tenderness to respond in a loving manner. However, don't go into the conversation expecting immediate understanding or forgiveness. Your fiancé may need time to work through emotions and think about what he or she hears.

6. As you talk with your fiancé, explain why you think it's important to share these parts of your past, but avoid sharing more than is necessary. Be careful about sharing too many explicit details, as this can give the one you love even more to overcome that isn't necessary for forgiveness and healing. It's important to use discretion and help your fiancé avoid unhealthy curiosity.

7. Give your fiancé the time he or she needs to process this new information. This may include hurt, anger, or even withdrawal.

8. If it becomes apparent that either of you cannot get beyond the hurt caused by relating this information, seek careful advice from trusted, mature Christians together or individually. Including a sex trauma therapist in this healing process might be necessary. If forgiveness and reconciliation cannot occur at this point, then delaying the wedding could be the wise decision. If the Holy Spirit—through prayer, fasting, the Bible, and counsel—continues to direct you toward marriage with your eyes wide open, you can trust Him to demonstrate His perfect strength for your repeated choices toward unconditional, godly love for each other. As Scripture tells us, "No one has ever seen God; if we love one another, God abides in us and his love is perfected in us. . . . Perfect love casts out fear" (1 John 4:12, 18).

If you are hearing a confession from your fiancé:

1. Make an effort to really hear what your fiancé is sharing. Ask yourself, *Why did he/she come to me with this?* Look beyond the past and its ugliness to the broken heart that is sharing.

2. Keep in mind your own brokenness and your own forgiveness before Jesus. Because we don't love perfectly and because we can feel that we "deserve the perfect person," we might be tempted to condemn another for a past failure, whereas God calls us to forgive each other.

Don't let pride prevent you from responding with love and forgiveness when your fiancé is willing to share mistakes or hurts from the past.

You might express ideas like, "Thank you so much for telling me and trusting me with something so hard to share. I still care about you, and you can feel safe sharing with me, even if I'm hurt or angry or don't know what I feel or what to do about this. God loves and forgives and accepts both of us unconditionally because of Jesus. We both need Him so deeply."

If you have significant concerns over what is shared, invite a mentor or counselor in before you decide to move forward or call off the marriage. Outside insight can help guide how you process your fiancé's past.

Summary

Sex can be amazing and it can be amazingly complicated. God designed sex to connect two people's souls and create and nurture an intimacy unlike any other. That's why He set loving boundaries around sex—to protect our holistic selves from fracturing apart and to help us pursue the naked-and-unashamed environment a gospel-centered marriage ought to provide. We pray this chapter has been an encouraging look at the preciousness of the gift of sex in marriage, and that you and your fiancé can enter into marriage in joyful anticipation (plus, tons of grace and understanding for each other) of God-honoring, delight-bringing sexual intimacy.

eight

LET'S TALK ABOUT RELATIONSHIPS WITH OTHERS

Meg is *very* close with her parents. And I get it—as I mentioned in chapter 5, my in-laws are wonderful—and I love that they have carried that bond her whole life. What I didn't necessarily expect, early on in our marriage, was what it might feel like for me if my new wife looked to them for help or comfort on an issue before or instead of me. It stung a little! Of course, she wasn't trying to exclude me or make me feel unvalued or unimportant—she was just relating to her caring, godly parents the same way she always had.

While dating, you might not have been focused as much on your partner's family and friends. Or, the dynamics might have been completely normal for two unmarried people. After marriage, though, it's natural and right for these relationships to change (at least a little). This can cause problems you didn't see coming if you haven't intentionally thought through how you'll navigate these changes as a couple.

Mutually agreed-upon boundaries that establish how you interact with family and friends directly affects the extent of health, connection, and unity in a marriage.

A lack of communication in this area or a misunderstanding of your new norms as a couple can cause significant friction with your spouse and simultaneously hurt others you've been close with for a long time. However, freedom can be found when there is ample conversation about how these relationships will be handled after you are married.

Family

Because we all come from a variety of backgrounds, cultures, ethnicities, socioeconomic levels, etc., it can be quite difficult to prescribe what your future relationships with family should look like. Perhaps you have grown up very close to your immediate family, and you cannot fathom their involvement in your life decreasing once you get married. Or maybe the opposite is true, and not much of anything will change with your family once you get married. Or your relationship with your family could be anywhere in varied spectrum of scenarios. Regardless of your background, it is essential that you as an engaged couple talk about what your expectations are for family involvement in your lives going forward.

It's impossible to have *every* essential conversation about future family involvement before the wedding because, as you'll find out, much will come up along the way after you're married. Not every problem or possible challenge can be foreseen. However, there's still much that can be discussed in a helpful way now, as you are preparing for life together.

Take some time to answer the following four questions individually, and once you've finished, share your answers with each other.

Family Expectations

1. How many times per week do you desire or plan to interact with your family (parents or caregivers/siblings/etc.)?

   In-person visit at their home: _____

   Call (lengthy conversation): _____

   In-person visit in our home: _____

   Other in-person interactions: _____

2. How many times per month do you desire or plan to spend at least one day (like on a weekend) with your family, and what do you expect that time will look like when you're all together?

_____

_____

_____

3. What are your expectations for how we will include your family in celebrating holidays and birthdays?

_____

_____

_____

4. When something major happens in life, good or bad, this is who I reach out to first in my family:

_____

_____

Receive, Leave, and Cleave

The reason we asked you to share some of your expectations with your fiancé before digging into some biblical principles is that, acknowledged or not, there is already a preexisting set of norms that you'll bring into your marriage.

We talked about this already in the "Let's Talk about Our Hopes" chapter, but we want now to dig a bit deeper and consider what the Bible has to say about the fundamental nature of Christian marriage and how we ought to live out our marriages in a way that pleases God and is best for us.

God Calls You to Receive Your Spouse

> So the Lord God caused a deep sleep to fall upon the man, and while he slept took one of his ribs and closed up its place with flesh. And the rib that the Lord God had taken from the man he made into a woman and brought her to the man.
>
> Genesis 2:21–22

Once God had made Adam "a helper suitable for him" (Genesis 2:18 NIV), one question remained: What would Adam's response be? Remember that he had been busy naming the animals when God put him under a deep sleep, but when he awoke, his wife was in front of him. Adam knew nothing about her other than that she had come from God.

So, how did he respond? "Then the man said, 'This at last is bone of my bones and flesh of my flesh; she shall be called Woman, because she was taken out of Man'" (Genesis 2:23).

Adam was obviously enthusiastic about what had just happened, and he broke into poetry over the gift God had given to him. His focus was on God's flawless character, not on Eve's performance. He knew God, and he knew that God could be trusted. Adam gladly *received* Eve because he knew she was from God. Adam's faith in God enabled him to receive her as God's gift for him.

Not for lack of wanting, none of us woke up to find a spouse designed especially for us. We get to choose, while trusting that God works through even our foolish or sinful choices, or others': "As for you, you meant evil against me, but God meant it for good" (Genesis 50:20). It's possible that, once married, you may occasionally entertain some doubts: *What if I made a mistake? What if there is someone better for me out there?* But once you've said "I do," there's no doubt that God has given your spouse to you to love for better or for worse.

5. Complete the following sentence. If when we are married, my spouse truly is "from God," then receiving him or her looks like:

_____

_____

In marriage, we are called to receive our spouse, including their strengths and weaknesses. We must come to a point where we ask ourselves, *Will I unconditionally accept him/her? Will I look beyond physical attractiveness and appealing qualities to God, who is the provider and who knows what He's doing?*

Receiving your spouse is not just a decision you make when reciting your wedding vows. It requires an attitude of *continual acceptance* throughout your marriage. When we pursue that, we beautifully reflect the acceptance we continually receive from God by His undeserved kindness, not at all dependent on what we do: "Welcome one another as Christ has welcomed you, for the glory of God" (Romans 15:7).

In the months and years after the wedding, each of you will become more and more aware of your respective weaknesses and faults. By God's Spirit, the more you remember your responsibility to receive each other as God's provision, the stronger your marriage will be.

Does this mean permitting any form of abuse or manipulation, or turning a blind eye if a spouse is flirting with someone else, or succumbing to an addiction, or losing it with the kids, or lying about taxes? No way! "If anyone is caught in any transgression, you who are spiritual should restore him in a spirit of gentleness" (Galatians 6:1). Christian love is a kind that helps each other toward holiness, that speaks the truth in love (Ephesians 4:15).

6. If one of you somehow fell into a pattern of not receiving your spouse unconditionally, what could your marriage look like in, say, five or ten years?

God Calls You to Leave Your Parents

Look a little further on in the Genesis passage to uncover more of God's plan for marriage:

> Therefore shall a man leave his father and his mother, and shall cleave unto his wife: and they shall be one flesh.
>
> Genesis 2:24 KJV

As children, we are dependent upon our parents or caregivers for material and nonmaterial things. Our parents or caregivers have the responsibility of providing food, shelter, and clothing, as well as emotional stability, wise values, and spiritual guidance. As we grow older, our dependance on them changes—part of their job is to prepare us for life as Christ-following adults.

You know that part in a traditional wedding ceremony when, having walked his daughter down the aisle, the father takes her hands and places them in her new husband's? That physical act is a picture of how the *posture* of the married couple shifts toward each other. Sometimes later in the service, the parents might return to the altar to place their hands upon the shoulders of their children—another beautiful picture of how parents continue to support not just their child anymore but the new one-flesh entity of their child and child's spouse.

We should always honor our parents (see Exodus 20:12), but as we enter into adulthood, and certainly into marriage, *leaving* them is punctuated. Whereas as children we were called to obey and our dependence upon them was right and necessary, we must lean into obeying and depending on the Lord, as well as the healthy interdependence we are called to build as husband and wife.

This posture shift of "leaving father and mother . . . to become one flesh" will likely involve two aspects:

Primary Dependency

Because God wants spouses—as two unique people choosing one-flesh unity—to journey together through life for His glory, you and your spouse will practice healthy interdependence. A child receives what they need from their parents. You and your spouse will *rely on each other*. You'll need each other, in a way you won't need any other human person, to follow whatever path God lays out for you.

Obedience versus Respect

As children, we're fully expected to obey our parents. They act as our very necessary guides to teach us about life and godliness. In adulthood, we are responsible ourselves. In marriage, our responsibility before God is to obey Him above all, and because we are now one flesh in marriage, we do that together with a spouse. We can still enjoy, care for, and be cared for by our parents, and shifting our posture from our parents to our spouses doesn't mean we cut our families out of our new lives. We seek to be there for our parents and respect them, and we're incredibly grateful they're there for us, too. It only means that our relationships with our families should never undermine our allegiance to God and our one-flesh unity with our spouse.

7. In your own words, write a brief description of what "a man shall leave his father and mother" practically looks like.

_____

_____

_____

_____

8. What are some ways people may fail to shift primary dependance away from their parents after they are married?

_____

_____

_____

_____

9. What are some ways people may fail to shift from a posture of obedience to a posture of respect?

_____

_____

_____

_____

10. As you consider "leaving" your parents or caregivers, which of the two posture shifts will be the most difficult for you to make or maintain? Why?

_____

_____

_____

_____

11. In your opinion, which of the two shifts will be the most difficult for your fiancé to make or maintain?

_____

_____

_____

_____

12. Are there any ways that you think your parents or caregivers, or your fiancé's, will find it difficult to let you "leave"?

_____

_____

_____

God Calls You to Cleave to Your Spouse

Genesis 2:24 tells us that after leaving his parents, a man shall "cleave to his wife." Now, *cleave* isn't a word we use everyday; it basically means to join, unite, adhere, or stick like glue. In other words, it's a permanent bond, not meant to be broken.

On your wedding day, you will participate with your spouse in one of the most solemn pledges ever given to humankind—the covenant of marriage. This is a lifelong commitment, a promise not just between two people but between a man and a woman and God. It involves *at least* three important promises:

To stay married throughout your lives

To faithfully love and care for each other no matter what

To maintain sexual and emotional fidelity

When you enter into marriage, you do so with the understanding that you fully intend to keep your vows. This sacred commitment directly correlates to the level of security in your marriage relationship. A partial commitment creates fear and distrust, hamstringing honesty, dependence, and teamwork, and leaves room for your marriage to isolate or begin to fail.

Love is more than a feeling. If it were only a feeling, we would fall in and out of love often because we're all selfish by nature. Love can't be sustained by feelings or emotions. And when you think about it, this is at the heart of commitment. Commitment is the unconditional, irrevocable promise to always be there. It is the resolute conviction of your will to stick to that person for life.

Covenant commitment to a person in marriage is meant to be a reflection of God's covenant commitment to us. He will never leave us or forsake us. He will always love us, despite our chronic ability to fail. He brims over with love and compassion toward us, and we reflect that commitment through faithfulness to each other in marriage.

When you display this kind of commitment to each other, you display God's good purposes for the covenant of marriage. Your relationship becomes a witness to the world of God's character. Your unconditional commitment to each other radiates God's unconditional commitment in a world of broken promises and fractured relationships. How beautiful is that?!

13. What does it mean to be a person of your word? If you claim to be a Christian, why is a covenant so important?

_____

_____

_____

_____

14. Why are receiving, leaving, and cleaving exciting to you? What about these seems difficult?

_____

_____

_____

_____

All in all, your new marriage is the start-up of a new family. From "I do" on, when you say, "my family," you'll be speaking *primarily* of your spouse rather than the family of your upbringing. That's new, right? And while leaving your parents or caregivers and cleaving to your husband or wife will take some getting used to, it's the all-in path to God's way of thriving in your covenant commitment.

In-Laws

Another new dynamic you'll experience as a married person is . . . in-laws, which could include parents or caregivers, siblings, grandparents, aunts, uncles, cousins, etc. After the ceremony, his or her family will become your family. For some people, it's wonderful to gain in-laws, and for others, it's difficult. And for many, it's a little of both.

Don't downplay your in-laws' impact on your new marriage. Understand it. Plan for it. Answer the following questions on your own, and then come back together and share your responses with your fiancé.

15. How much time do you desire to spend with your future in-laws?

16. How would you feel about your in-laws stopping by your home unannounced?

17. Would you want your in-laws to give you advice regarding money? Why or why not?

18. What is the best way for you to communicate respect and love to your future in-laws?

Regardless of your relationships with your future in-laws, you can know that if God is calling you to your fiancé, He's calling you to his or her family, too. God's perfectly orchestrated plan has ushered them purposefully into your life, so look at them with love and acceptance. We're not saying don't have any boundaries, but remember that your treatment of them could add happiness to their lives as well as your own, and could develop into opportunities to reflect Christ.

Friends

> This is my commandment, that you love one another as I have loved you. Greater love has no one than this, that someone lay down his life for his friends.
>
> John 15:12–13

One of the more potentially tricky relationship connections you'll need to navigate after you get married is that of your existing friendships. It's not all that unusual for couples to get married and essentially cut off their other friendships, only to realize the mistake they've made a few months later, after the *newly* has worn off from *newlywed*. On the other hand, some couples marry without changing *anything* about how they relate to their respective friends, only to realize that their marriage is already suffering for lack of focused connection with their spouse.

But with some intentionality, you can live as married people who still have strong and healthy friendships.

Not to sound cliché, but your future husband or wife ideally will be your best friend. What other friend counts as "one flesh" (Genesis 2:25)? Still, your spouse cannot meet your every relationship need, so in addition to that unique friendship, other healthy friendships need to exist for both of you alongside your marriage. Everyone needs relational connections with other friends to talk with, laugh with, cry with, and listen to.

One of the most valuable assets you can have as a married person is a core group of close friends of the same sex who you share your "deepest and darkest" with. People you trust, care about, and count on to speak wisdom into your life, and rely on to call you out when you need it. They can be a lifeline of God's tenderness when you need wisdom, and a refreshing breath when you need a good laugh. Human beings are made by God as relational creatures, so to starve yourself of deep, godly friendships just because you are now married is detrimental.

Discerning how to spend your time and energy with your friends after you get married is crucial, especially as newlyweds. Are there ways you might need to adjust your regular guys' or ladies' nights to prioritize your marriage? It's important to talk about your expectations as a couple in an effort to avoid disappointment or hurt feelings. Answer the following questions on your own, and then come back together with your fiancé and share your answers with each other.

19. How often would you like to spend time with just your friends once you are married?

20. How often will you want your spouse to spend time with his or her friends?

21. What do you think you'd be most likely to do after you are married—spend too much time with your friends or too little?

_____

_____

_____

22. What kinds of healthy boundaries do you need to discuss concerning your *individual* friends and how involved they will be in your lives?

_____

_____

_____

23. What conversations need to happen with your friends to help them understand that your life is about to change and your first priority (after God) will be your spouse?

_____

_____

_____

24. After you get married, how can you and your spouse best communicate your commitment to your friends and your love for them?

_____

_____

_____

Summary

Hopefully, your family and friends will be a great support and strength to your upcoming marriage. Having people who are *for you* and *for your marriage* is a profound gift. And remember, one of God's purposes of marriage is for a husband and wife to help each other love God and love others in even more powerful, beautiful ways. Your marriage can be an encouragement and gift to your loved ones, as well. Beginning and maintaining good communication with your spouse and loved ones can open the door to a lifetime of rich, life-giving relationships.

nine

LET'S TALK ABOUT FAITH

There's a question we want you and your fiancé to soberly consider: "Are we going in the same spiritual direction?" In other words, are both of you authentic Christians who are pursuing God and spiritual maturity?

Because marriage is a spiritual relationship, your spiritual compatibility will influence the quality of your relationship more than any other factor. Consider this passage from 2 Corinthians 6:14–15:

> Do not be unequally yoked with unbelievers. For what partnership has righteousness with lawlessness? Or what fellowship has light with darkness? What accord has Christ with Belial? Or what portion does a believer share with an unbeliever?

Most of us are only familiar with egg *yolks*, so this passage can sound pretty strange. A yoke is a wooden crosspiece that is fastened over the necks of two animals (typically oxen) and attached to a plow or cart that they pull as a team. According to Deuteronomy 22:10, God's people weren't allowed to yoke, say, a donkey and an ox because if one animal was stronger than the other, one was often pulling the weight while the other couldn't keep up. Plus the plow would cut through the ground erratically, and sometimes ineffectively, because the two animals were out of sync. It was an inhumane match of ability and disposition that didn't lead to a team being happy and effective in their work together.

Tracking with this metaphor, if Jesus is at the center of your life, why would you want to be hitched to someone who has nothing in common with you spiritually? If you are "unequally yoked" in your marriage, sooner or later you'll pull against each other, and that will lead to heartbreak, grief, and frustration.

Second Corinthians 6:14–15 warns Christians about building their lives with someone who has clashing values and goals. Building relationships on God's values, trust, and love is essential. Another warning is given in James: "Do you not know that friendship with the world is hostility toward God? Therefore whoever wants to be a friend of the world makes himself an enemy of God" (James 4:4 NASB). Trust me, it can be hard enough to prevent our hearts from being lured into "loving the world" (being controlled by pride, greed, and divisiveness) even when your spouse is *also* pursuing God and encouraging you. God created marriage, and its maximum satisfaction can only be found when you both have a growing relationship with Him.

When Christians marry non-Christians, they usually experience a growing, unique frustration after marriage because:

They are unable to discuss the most precious, intimate part of their life with their spouse.

They often have conflicting goals and expectations.

They may clash over the values they teach their kids.

They will likely have differing circles of friends.

They can have difficulty communicating and resolving conflict because of different core values in their lives.

If one of you is a Christ follower and the other is not, you need to consider how deeply this will affect your marriage. It's bigger than a hobby you wish your spouse enjoyed: Following Jesus imprints itself into every aspect of our lives. As much as you may love each other and envision a beautiful life together, if this is your situation, we'd like to gently suggest some thoughtful time on this very tough question: Should the two of you get married?

Commitment to Spiritual Growth

> Do not love the world or the things in the world. If anyone loves the world, the love of the Father is not in him.
>
> 1 John 2:15

You may both have decided to follow Christ, but if one of you is more focused on loving the world rather than loving God, you will experience many of the same conflicts as a Christian and non-Christian. Your goals and values will differ. Your lives are going in different directions, serving different bosses.

If you are both growing in Christ, however, you'll be able experience a particular exhilaration and teamwork in your marriage.

Running coaches usually encourage their long-distance runners to train in groups rather than as individuals, because when they're in a group, runners encourage one another to push past their weariness and pain. In fact, a runner may run faster in a group than alone, and even feel less fatigued. In the same way, two people who share the same commitment to God can encourage and help each other to keep their eyes on Christ as they "run with endurance" (Hebrews 12:1) and push each other toward spiritual closeness and surging growth with Him.

1. List some words or phrases that describe your current relationship with Christ.

   _____

   _____

   _____

   _____

2. Indicate whether you agree or disagree with this statement as you think about your fiancé, and why: "Our relationship is solidly built on Christ."

   _____

   _____

141

_____

_____

To further evaluate this area of your spiritual compatibility, ask yourself questions such as:

Do both of us share the same desire to know and please God?

Do I have any sense that one of us is putting on a facade of spiritual commitment?

Do our actions back up our words? Do we both have a consistent track record of this?

Do we both consistently display a desire to obey God in everything?

What priority does each of us place on serving other people?

Are we both seeking to follow God's direction and His kingdom before anything else (Matthew 6:33)?

3. How would you describe your spiritual compatibility right now?

_____

_____

_____

_____

4. What changes would need to occur in you personally to increase your spiritual compatibility? What opportunities do you see for growth in your fiancé to increase your spiritual compatibility?

_____

_____

_____

_____

Growing Together

"What is God's will for my life?" Many people ask this very good question at various points in their lives. But an *even better* question would be, "How does my life fit into God's will and what He's already doing in the world?"

The second question shifts the focus to the appropriate place—onto God instead of ourselves. It assumes that God is moving and working in the world, and that He's most important. He is in charge, and whatever He calls us to do, we do, knowing that He will care for us along the way.

Of course, it's impossible to say *how* God will actually care for us along the way, since everyone's life is different, but it's safe to trust that He will. Even a cursory approach to reading the Bible reveals that God is very attentive throughout life. He's present, pervasive, and personal. He's already working and active in this world, and you and your fiancé will want to repeatedly consider, "How is our marriage fitting into God's will, which is to ultimately bring God glory?"

It's critical that you as a couple pursue spiritual growth together alongside your individual growth. Personal growth with the Lord often looks like private time alone with God, reading Scripture, prayer, worship, etc. Spiritual maturity as a couple, however, is something that can be a bit more challenging because there are two people involved with two sets of ideas, preferences, struggles, and ways of processing growth.

You'll find, though, that growing together spiritually as a married couple is one of the most refreshing and rewarding experiences you can have. Deepening your relationship with the Lord alongside your best friend for years upon years is one of the most generous gifts God gives.

Collective growth as a married couple can look different ways: studying a book of the Bible together, reading a Christian book together and discussing it, praying together, exercising hospitality, listening to or watching sermons together and then sharing your notes and thoughts, etc. There are so many ways a married couple can discover new heights of spiritual development alongside each other—they simply need to collectively commit to it, stay disciplined in the process, and ask the Spirit of God to create the growth in their lives together.

Setting up a pattern of regular time together dedicated to your collective spiritual growth will foster a good habit and healthy norm in your marriage that will produce fruit for decades to come (check out John 15:8).

5. Brainstorm a list of ways you and your future spouse can intentionally run toward spiritual maturity after you get married. Think of both general and specific ways.

_____

_____

_____

_____

6. Keeping in mind what you know now about each other and what your plans are once you get married, list some of the potential roadblocks to your collective spiritual maturity.

_____

_____

_____

_____

God Himself Makes It Possible

When it comes to our goals for consistent spiritual growth and development, we can lack the power to persevere. Willing our way into spiritual maturity doesn't get the job done. When we try to go toe-to-toe with the behemoth that is our own sinful bent, our own strength will give out before the fight's over. But *with God* all things are possible (Genesis 18:14; Matthew 19:26; Luke 1:37).

As Christians, we trust God to work in us and bring life to the dead and weak areas of our lives. And even though buckling down and trying harder isn't the answer, we do have a role in our spiritual growth. In the same way you can't *make* sleep come at night, you can still lie there with the lights off—putting yourself in a good position for it to come. We cooperate with Him through obedience and trust. Understanding and living this out will change your life and your marriage.

7. What are some areas in your Christian life that you'd really like to see strengthened?

_____

_____

_____

_____

8. When welcoming the Holy Spirit to make spiritual growth possible in your marriage, take a moment to think about what your relationship will look like as *love, joy, peace, patience, kindness, goodness, faithfulness, gentleness, and self-control* develop more fully in you as a husband or wife.

   Now, write out a prayer asking God to do the work of transforming you to be more like Jesus, shaping your marriage into the best it can be by the life-changing power of His Spirit.

_____

_____

_____

_____

_____

_____

_____

_____

ten

LET'S TALK ABOUT THE LONG HAUL

Are you excited about the future? It probably looks pretty bright from where you're sitting right now. After all, you're making plans to spend it with the love of your life.

This final conversation guide concentrates on the long view of your marriage and what you can do to make your marriage a strong and happy one for the years ahead.

We'll direct this conversation toward three of the best practices of couples who experience that connected unity over the long haul:

- Resolving conflict intentionally
- Inviting others into your journey
- Pursuing a purpose bigger than your own happiness

Resolving Conflict Intentionally

Romantic feelings are intoxicating and a true gift from God to a newly married couple. Appreciate them. Enjoy them. However, we all know that romance can be fickle—you can be swimming in it one day, and the next feel as if your relationship has been completely drained of it.

While you are in this current stage as an engaged couple, happily getting ready for marriage, we don't want you to get blindsided by the probability that your excitement may wane, come back, and then wane again. Repeat.

But there is good news. Christians don't build their marriages on romance but on Jesus. Romance is great, and you definitely want it in your marriage, but it's unreliable as your foundation. Studies indicate that the effervescent wash of brain chemicals lasts two years, max.

So look to your foundation first—the unchanging love of Christ—and then move into the practicalities of what to do when conflict arises.

Based on our upbringing, family history, temperament, and so on, we all approach resolving conflict in different ways. As Christians, though, let's make a habit of turning first to God's Word.

1. What does the following verse have to say about resolving conflict?

   Be angry and do not sin; do not let the sun go down on your anger.

   Ephesians 4:26

   Resolving conflict looks like . . .

   _____

   _____

   _____

   _____

2. What happens when couples don't apply this principle? (Note: Some conflicts get irrational late into the night. The general principle is to not stay angry with your spouse. Sometimes stepping back and cooling off is necessary and safe, and that might mean resolving the conflict the next day.)

   _____

   _____

   _____

   _____

Maybe you already see yourselves reacting to conflict in different ways, like these:

- *Fight to Win*: This is the "I win, you lose" or "I must defend what's right—and I'm right" position. You may seek to dominate, and personal relationships can matter less in the moment than the need to win.

- *Withdraw*: You seek to avoid conflict and its discomfort, saying, "I'm uncomfortable, so I'll get out." You may see little hope of resolving the conflict in beneficial ways, or you lack the strength to confront it. Some who take this approach cope by giving their spouse the silent treatment or pulling back in various forms of intimacy or care. (Note: Don't confuse this with self-regulation, internal processing, creating space, or trauma responses like fight, flight, freeze, or fawn. Sometimes withdrawal is necessary, as long as it's communicated: "I need time to think about this. Can we please talk about this [at a specific time]?" Those boundaries need to be respected when requested.)

- *Yield*: You assume it is better to go along with the other person's demands than to risk a confrontation. Rather than risking another argument, you say in essence, "Whatever you want is fine." A safe feeling through the *appearance of peace* is more important than a close relationship and peace on the other side of conflict.

- *Lovingly Resolve*: You commit to resolving the conflict by taking steps to carefully and sensitively discuss the issue. Resolving a conflict requires a particular attitude—one of humility, of placing the health of the relationship at a higher priority than the conflict itself. Conflict is a chance to better understand each other's values, grow in character, and honor God by mimicking what Christ did for us in our conflict with Him. You value your relationship more than winning, retreating, or feeling comfortable.

With the first three styles, you create as many problems as you solve. Fighting to win, withdrawing, or yielding may allow you a temporary break from the conflict at hand, but you haven't really dealt with the emotions the conflict has sparked—the hurt, the resentment, the fear, and the anger. Only when you approach each other in a loving way will you resolve a conflict.

3. What does the following verse have to say about resolving conflict?

   Be kind to one another, tenderhearted, forgiving one another, as God in Christ forgave you.

   Ephesians 4:32

   Resolving conflict means . . .

   _____

   _____

   _____

   _____

4. What can happen in a relationship when this principle is not applied?

   _____

   _____

   _____

   _____

Resolving conflict also requires forgiveness—giving up the right to punish the one who has wronged you and doing good to them instead. This is the outgrowth of the Christian life—that we can pursue healing in our relationships with others in the same way Christ healed our relationship with Him by laying down His anger, closing the gap, and extending forgiveness. I won't lie, this can be *hard*. I find that if I'm struggling to authentically forgive Meg, it's a sign that I need some time to do business with God—to ask Him to remind me of just how great His mercy and love are for me, so I can extend mercy to my beloved, too.

Inviting Others into Your Journey

Back in chapter 5 (Let's Listen to Our People), we talked about the importance of getting "positive and reliable input from a trusted community." There will never come a season in your life or marriage when you will have all the answers or reach a level of self-sufficiency. God has made us to be interdependent, drawing life and wisdom from outside our own way of thinking. Using the analogy of a human body, He says ignoring our need for others is spiritual breakdown: "The eye cannot say to the hand, 'I have no need of you,' nor again the head to the feet, 'I have no need of you'" (1 Corinthians 12:21).

5. What do each of the following verses, all taken from the book of Proverbs, tell us about the value of seeking counsel?

> *Where there is no guidance, a people falls, but in an abundance of counselors there is safety.*
>
> *Proverbs 11:14*

> *Without counsel plans fail, but with many advisers they succeed.*
>
> *Proverbs 15:22*

> *For by wise guidance you can wage your war, and in abundance of counselors there is victory.*
>
> *Proverbs 24:6*

Seeking input from others can help us . . .

_____

_____

_____

_____

6. What have been some of the best pieces of advice you have received thus far in life related to dating, engagement, and marriage? How have they improved your relationship for the long haul?

_____

_____

_____

_____

7. What have been some of the best pieces of advice you have received thus far in life related to things *other than* dating, engagement, and marriage? How have they changed you for the better?

_____

_____

_____

_____

In chapter 5, we provided instructions and questions for interviewing mentor couples. Again, this is a practice you could benefit from throughout the years—occasionally and intentionally seeking the input of couples who are further along in their marriage than you are. We urge you to do this interview on an annual basis, perhaps around your wedding anniversary. By asking good questions and listening to what these couples have to offer, you will increase the safety (Proverbs 11:14), success (Proverbs 15:22), and victory (Proverbs 24:6) in your marriage.

You could also ask questions like these:

- What lessons have you learned about keeping love alive over the long haul?

- Where do you go for advice on marriage and family?

- What are some habits that have helped the two of you stay close?

- Are there any things you wish you would have started earlier in your marriage? What are they?

- Do you have any advice for resolving conflict?

- What are some mistakes you see couples making, and what can we do to avoid these mistakes?

- Tell us about something you weren't expecting in the first five years of your marriage. How did you deal with it?

- (If they have children) How did having children change your relationship dynamic? Is there anything that would have helped you be better prepared for that stage of your marriage?

A key thought to keep in mind: *Be intentional*. Proactively seeking the counsel and involvement of others will protect you from taking each other for granted and will keep you on the same course. With that in mind . . .

8. What couple(s) do we want to include in our first "marriage review"? (List some potential names here.)

_____

_____

There's a lot to be said for simply paying attention to other marriages—making note of things you may want to avoid or pursue. Some of the best things we learned from others didn't come from explicit advice, but by simply observing couples we respect. Over the course of your marriage, many different couples will cross your path, but intentional time with other couples who are pursuing God will bless your marriage for the long haul.

Pursuing a Purpose Bigger Than Your Own Happiness

We wholeheartedly affirm you for putting in the work of preparing well and for your desire to love each other faithfully. We hope your love will grow and flourish for years to come.

If you think there is a *but* coming, you are correct. And here it is: *But,* we know that one of the most rewarding goals for your marriage is to make it about more than *your marriage.*

Certainly God has brought the two of you together to enjoy the intimate experiences of giving and receiving love—the shared secrets, the private jokes, the flirtatious looks you pass back and forth, the sharing of a bed. Yet just as God told Adam and Eve to "fill the earth and subdue it, and have dominion over the fish of the sea and over the birds of the heavens and over every living thing that moves on the earth" (Genesis 1:28), so He has purposes for you, as a couple, that will take you outside the walls of your home and into the world. He has good work for you to do together.

9. Read the verse below. Talk about some of the "good works" you would like to accomplish together as a couple. What do you dream about doing to make a difference in the world?

> *For we are his workmanship, created in Christ Jesus for good works, which God prepared beforehand, that we should walk in them.*
>
> *Ephesians 2:10*

_____

_____

_____

_____

10. Take a few minutes to affirm each other, specifically stating some of the character qualities, skills, etc. you see in your fiancé that you believe God wants to use to help others.

_____

_____

_____

_____

God operates differently than we do. We may think that the way to grow in connectedness and oneness of spirit is to give each other undivided attention, thinking only of others when it is absolutely necessary, and then only for a short time. But God has designed marriage to make an impact. The couples who enjoy greater oneness are those who live for purposes beyond their own happiness.

As you prepare for marriage, think about what it will mean to the world that on a certain day in a certain year in a certain place, a certain man and a certain woman said, "I do." Think about the statement you want your relationship to make fifty years from now, the imprint you hope to leave on the lives you touch. This will be your legacy. And it starts now.

EPILOGUE

You know that preparing for marriage isn't a one-and-done event. There's no such thing as taking the course, passing the test, checking the box, and then settling in for a lifetime of marital bliss—sometimes I wish there were! You must keep talking with each other and keep listening. Keep asking to be filled with God's mercy, so that it will overflow to your soon-to-be spouse. Some curveballs are going to be thrown at you in the days, weeks, months, years, and decades to come, and you'll need to remember that God is *for you*.

Proverbs 16:4 reminds us, "The Lord has made everything for its purpose, even the wicked for the day of trouble." Good times will be plentiful, and difficult times will be, too, but never forget that there is a great God who can use both the good and the bad to strengthen your connection, deepen your love, and build your faith. He knows *exactly* what He's doing in your lives, and because He is good and loving, you can always trust that nothing is beyond His care or control.

Only God knows the unique pleasure and pain you will face as husband and wife, but you can draw courage and hope—in both the peace and the chaos—because He cares for you. The cross of Jesus Christ is all the evidence you'll ever need to know that God loves you, He is for you, and He died to be in relationship with you.

Let your marriage be a living testament to this Good News. Drink it in daily, live it passionately, and receive His gifts humbly, knowing that you and your spouse are held in His perfect hands.

ADDITIONAL RESOURCES

For additional copies of the worksheet, survey, question-naire, and conversation guides, scan this QR code:

You can also find tips for requesting mentors and a free mentor's guide available online.

David and **Meg Robbins** are passionate about integrating faith and family while equipping people to invest in their communities. David became the President of FamilyLife in 2017. The Robbinses have served in a variety of ministry roles over the years in western Europe and as a National Director for Cru's Campus Field Ministry.

Before FamilyLife, the Robbinses lived in Manhattan, where they helped launch an initiative with Cru for twenty-somethings. Their desire is to leverage FamilyLife's resources to engage new audiences and generations to come.

David and Meg, married in 2001, currently live in Orlando, Florida, with their four children.